PASSIONATE
for JUSTICE

IDA B. WELLS

AS PROPHET FOR OUR TIME

CATHERINE MEEKS & NIBS STROUPE

FOREWORD BY STACEY ABRAMS

CHURCH
PUBLISHING
INCORPORATED

Church Publishing
19 East 34th Street
New York, NY 10016
www.churchpublishing.org

Cover photo courtesy of the University of Chicago Library, Special Collections Research Center. Digital Reproduction: Existing Archival Photographic Collection (apf1-08641 Ida B. Wells Formal #5).

Cover design by Marc Whitaker, MTWdesign
Typeset by Rose Design

A record of this book is available from the Library of Congress.

ISBN-13: 978-1-64065-160-9 (pbk.)
ISBN-13: 978-1-64065-161-6 (ebook)

Contents

Foreword

The story of America has no finer an example of perseverance, brilliance, and accomplishment than Ida B. Wells. She valiantly navigated a path of courage and strength and trumpeted the call to justice and equality, setting an example that continues to resonate for me and millions of others. Born into slavery in Mississippi, the state where I was raised, she saw the promise of Reconstruction and survived the scourge of white supremacy that followed. Despite a nation that ignored her humanity and shunned her potential, she understood that her capacity stretched deeper and wider than the definitions of white supremacy and of patriarchy. Like Harriet Tubman and Sojourner Truth, she crafted her own narrative, and in so doing became a clarion for our soul's deepest ambitions—justice.

A journalist, scholar, and activist, she wove together the ability to investigate and animate issues that robbed blacks of full participation in the citizenship guaranteed by the 13th, 14th and 15th Amendments. In 1892, when white men lynched her good friend Tom Moss in Memphis, she confronted the racism that sought to legitimize murder by vigilantes. She decried lynching and, moreover, demanded action from leaders who failed to protect their citizens. So affecting were her calls to action, her newspaper offices in Memphis were blown up. Though exiled from the South for more than twenty years, Wells became emboldened rather than silenced by the attack. The tenacity, ferocity, and dedication to justice of this former slave girl from rural Mississippi challenged the moral core of America, and her strategic vision for change transformed the lives of millions.

From co-founding the NAACP to producing a compendium of investigations that shocked the conscience of leaders, she redefined what leadership could and should look like. In particular, she furthered the role of women in the fight for justice, and she led without apology in an era when the words of women were not expected to be heard and where black women were summarily dismissed. Ida B. Wells refused to be dismissed.

Because of the witness and work of Ida Wells and those she girded for the fight, we as a nation have made critical progress. Yet, we find ourselves at a crucial turning point in our history, when the forces that sought to silence her and to reestablish oppression seem to gain strength each day. From the tragedy of family separations to the glib invocation of nativism, those charged with maintaining our progress have instead reignited the most infernal instincts of the past. In these moments, *Passionate for Justice* serves as a welcome and timely reminder of power of witness in our nation's history. I am grateful to Nibs Stroupe and Catherine Meeks for bringing forth this testimony to the life and ministry of Ida Wells. In this work, they reflect upon the power of Wells's life, as well as the dynamic of race and gender that sought to limit her and continues to constrict access into the present age.

I have been awed by Reverend Stroupe during his long and effective ministry at multicultural Oakhurst Presbyterian Church, where he met scripture with action. Together, with the scholarship and insight of Dr. Meeks, they have produced this critical work to help revive the heroism of Ida Wells, not only restoring our understanding of her unflinching example but reminding each of us to find our place in the perennial fight for justice. Through their exposition, we rediscover a model for diminishing those forces of repression and oppression in our individual and communal lives. In her honor, we are called to acknowledge the depth of those oppressive powers in our time, and to be like Wells—to seek a new way of liberty and justice for all.

Ida Wells confronted the evils of her time with a determination to compel America to live up to its highest ideals. Her example continues to guide the work of millions, including my own, as we in our own ways work to reaffirm the humanity of all and the potential for more. I applaud Nibs and Catherine for their efforts, a robust inquiry that produced such a transformative statement about the meaning of Wells's life for the twenty-first century. They honor the life of Ida B. Wells, a life carved out of the hardscrabble ground of slavery, white supremacy and oppression of women, especially black women. In *Passionate for Justice*, we find a compass that points us to the future, where we can each give voice and action to justice, equity, and life-giving community. Ida Wells would have had it no other way.

—Stacey Abrams
2018 Democratic Nominee for Governor of Georgia
Founder of Fair Fight Action
Founder of Fair Count
New York Times Bestselling Author of *Lead from the Outside*

An Introduction to Ida B. Wells from Her Great-Granddaughter

My great-grandmother Ida Bell Wells-Barnett (aka Ida B. Wells) spent almost fifty years of her life fighting for equality and justice during a period of history that spanned from the Civil War to the Great Depression. Through the writing of articles and pamphlets, plus delivering hundreds of speeches across the United States and the United Kingdom, she chronicled in great detail the atrocities and frequency of lynching that were used to terrorize the African American community. She co-founded and worked with several civil rights organizations that focused on both racial, gender, and economic equity. Not only did she work with some of the most well-known leaders of her time, but also interacted with the less fortunate on a personal level. She visited prisoners, worked as a probation officer, and created housing for Southern migrants.

Regardless of the personal sacrifice that was involved in her work, she was focused on fighting for the betterment of a country even though, as an African American and a woman, she faced discrimination on multiple fronts. She lived through some of the more violent and lawless times in American history. She put herself in dangerous situations in order to investigate the details of devastating riots. And because of her revealing the truth, calling out exact names of people, and encouraging disenfranchised people to fight back against the establishment, her own life was threatened. Despite the danger, criticism, and marginalization she faced, she somehow drew on a higher power and an inner strength to keep going—many times alone.

As our country experiences efforts to divide and oppress people based on race, religion, gender, or economic class, the life and decades and we are grateful to continue to have the courage to ask ourselves that question even though we have caught few glimpses of the answer. Thus, here we are two Arkansans, one African American female and one white male, taking a look at one of the most powerful women in our historical record through our respective lenses. Nibs is correct that this is not a book that a white man should have tried to write alone and I think that the conversation in this book has been enriched by our writing it together; Wells invites us into spaces that we might prefer to avoid on our own. It is critically important for all people, whether white or people of color, to learn how to have honest conversations about issues of race without seeing the difficult parts of those conversations as an invitation to vacate the path to healing. We have been able to engage one another in ways that would not have happened if we had been working on this book alone. We were both enriched and challenged by working together and offer this book to all of the readers with the hope that it will have a similar enriching effect.

We hope that the conversations that we have forged both in the words of the text and in our own hearts will be a source of encouragement, challenge, and example to all who read this book of ways that we can embrace the journey of racial healing. We hope that all who read this book will be challenged to be more than a half shade braver in the daily journey of working to be more open to that deep call from the heart to seek racial healing and wellness both as an individual and for the whole community.

—Catherine Meeks

CHAPTER 1

"To the Seeker of Truth"

Why Ida B. Wells? Because she did the work no one else would do. She kept showing up where she wasn't wanted. She worked with people who would work with her. She worked with people she didn't agree with and with whom she fought constantly. She worked for the betterment of a country that saw her doubly, as a black woman and as a second-class citizen. She lived through some of the darkest times in American history and did not live to see the biggest advancements that her daily work yielded in later decades. Yet she believed in herself, and in her ability to get things done, not just for herself, but for her fellow citizens.

Born in 1862 in Holly Springs, Mississippi, on the land owned by the man who "owned" her father and mother, Jim and Elizabeth Wells, Ida was born just before General Grant's troops captured Holly Springs in the Civil War. It would be a few more months before Union control of Holly Springs was solidified, but Ida Wells lived the early years of her life in slavery, yet under the oversight of the Union army. On the land where she was born, there now stands not the house of her former owner but rather a museum in her honor and memory.

And remembered she should be! Though born into slavery, she came to consciousness in the time of the Emancipation Proclamation and the defeat of the Confederacy in the Civil War. Thus, her primary definition was not "slave," not "property of white people"; her primary definition was daughter of God, woman held in slavery by those who professed the idea that all people are created equal. She never allowed that oppression narrative of slavery to enter her heart and consciousness and to become internalized. She never accepted the idea that she and her family were slaves because they were supposed to be slaves. She understood from the earliest stages that she was held as a slave because of the oppressive nature of the masters, and this consciousness made a huge difference in her life and in her imagination.

To gain deeper insight into the dilemma that confronted Wells and continues to serve as the foundation for white supremacy in the twenty-first century, we must travel through several treacherous paths in a short amount of time. This will include race and the naming of the races, as well as the perpetual crushing of people by pushing them to the margins. The modern system of race was not developed as a way to classify the different branches of the human family, but rather as a way of dominating the different branches of the human family. When it developed in the 1600s, as the Enlightenment and science began to grab hold of the European consciousness, it was rooted in the colonizing of the world. The purpose of the system of race was domination, not classification of the great diversity of the human family. If the dignity of the individual is essential in the Enlightenment age, how can we justify the exploitation of other humans from the colonies, if those individual humans have dignity too? The answer was to create a great gulf between those from Europe and those from other lands.

The answer became the system of race, as we currently know it. From the earliest systems of race, this purpose of domination seems evident. One of the greatest scientists of the Western world was Carolus Linnaeus, who developed the basic way of categorizing all living things. He emphasized the diversity of life and yet the commonality of life, and we still use his system today. He was also one of the early developers of the system of race. In 1738, he indicated four racial groups of humanity, and it is revealing to briefly review those categories:

Homo Europaeus—light, lively, inventive; ruled by rites
Homo Americanus—tenacious, contented, free; ruled by custom
Homo Asiaticus—stern, haughty, stingy; ruled by opinion
Homo After—cunning, slow, negligent; ruled by caprice.[1]

Here we see the beginnings of the system of race as we know it today—it is not meant to classify people in different branches of the human family. It is rather meant to indicate who should dominate and who should be dominated. We need a classification system that chronicles and notes the branches and the diversity of the human family, but the system of race is not that system.[2] This system works so that people classified as "white," especially white men, will internalize its approach and believe that we are superior. It also works so that all others will tend to internalize inferiority and believe that white males control almost all the power because they were ordained by God or by biology to do so. There are no significant biological or genetic differences between human beings; the system of race was developed to signify that there are such vast differences between human beings that those classified as "white" should be in power.

Ida Wells lived in the tensions and demonic powers of this system, but she was soaked in a spark of divinity that allowed her to see herself as God's child. She refused to abide by the attempts to strip her dignity in the post-Reconstruction days that reestablished slavery under the name of "neo-slavery," or "Jim Crow." She lived in the tension between equality and slavery in American history. No white person personifies this tension better than Thomas

---

1. Jacques Barzun, *Race: A Study in Superstition* (New York: Harper and Row, 1965), 35.

2. For fuller discussion of this development, see Nell Painter, *The History of White People* (New York: W. W. Norton and Company, 2010).

Jefferson. Fifty years after Linnaeus created his formula for the hierarchy of racial classifications, Jefferson gave his thoughts in 1785 in "Notes on Virginia."[3] In his earlier prose, Jefferson had helped to define the American identity: "We hold these truths to be self-evident, that all {men} are created equal." This radical idea of equality has been the driving force behind many of the justice movements in our country's history, including those who have insisted that women are included in this idea of self-evident equality. This powerful idea continues to motivate people of all classes and groups. Writing in 1785, however, Jefferson doesn't express the certainty of that idea of equality that fired the Declaration of Independence in 1776.

Jefferson waffles on equality because he wants to hold people as slaves while still professing belief in the revolutionary idea of equality. In "Notes on Virginia," he begins to see a hierarchy in this circle of equality, predating George Orwell's satirical concept that while all humans are created equal, some humans are more equal than others.[4] In his scientific analysis, Jefferson puts the "Homo sapiens Europaeus" on top of the racial ladder, with "the Indian" next and "blacks" on the bottom. While hoping to be objective and scientific, Jefferson admits that much more study is needed. Yet he must add this conclusion: "I advance it, therefore, as a suspicion only, that the blacks, whether originally a distinct race, or made distinct by time and circumstances, are inferior to the whites in the endowments both of body and mind."[5]

Although Jefferson later expresses misgivings about his dismissal of the equality of black people, his ruminations reflect the difficulty of all those who are classified as white in our society, whether in 1785 or 1985 or 2019. While committed to the

---

3. Thomas Jefferson, "Notes on the State of Virginia," in *Documents of American Prejudice*, ed. S. T. Joshi (New York: Basic Books, 1999), 11.

4. George Orwell, *Animal Farm* (New York: Harcourt, Brace and World, 1954).

5. Jefferson, "Notes on the State of Virginia," 11.

idea of equality, there are also distinct economic privileges to the inequality inherent in the system of race that places white folks on top of the ladder. For all of his misgivings about slavery, Jefferson benefitted immensely from it. At his death, his will freed only five of his slaves, all from the family conceived through his relationship with his slave Sally Hemmings.

While many who are classified as "white" would disavow the power of race and racism in our lives, the benefits cannot be denied. Jefferson shared this struggle, even as he quoted "scientific" evidence that seemed to verify that Africans were less equal than Europeans. If Africans were less than Europeans, then the "self-evident" clause of equality might not apply to them, and maybe, just maybe, holding them in bondage might be justified. In one form or another, throughout our history, "white" folk have gone through the same process as Jefferson did in order to justify the many privileges that come to those classified as "white" under the system of race. It was certainly true in the days of Ida Wells.

In 1875 in its last significant law for civil rights until 1957, the US Congress passed an act that forbade segregation on public accommodations. In 1883, the United States Supreme Court ruled the Civil Rights Act of 1875 unconstitutional, and the floodgates of segregation and reenslavement were open fully. In the spring of 1884, Ida Wells followed her usual pattern of purchasing a seat in the ladies' car on the train on a trip out of Memphis. After the train had pulled out, the conductor came to collect the tickets and then informed her that she would have to move to the car reserved for black people. Seventy-one years before Rosa Parks, she refused to give up her seat, and when he grabbed her and tried to pull her up from her seat, she bit his hand and braced herself not to move—no nonviolent resistance for her. He went to get male reinforcements, and it took three men to throw her off the train.

Undeterred, she took the railroad to court under Tennessee law, and the white judge who heard the case was a former Union soldier. He ruled in her favor and awarded her $500 in damages. She was thrilled with the victory, but it was short-lived. The railroad appealed to the Tennessee Supreme Court, and in 1887, they overturned the verdict. Ida Wells was crestfallen and wrote in her diary on April 11: "I had hoped for such great things from my suit for my people generally. I have firmly believed all along that the law was on our side and would, when we appealed to it, give us justice. I feel shorn of that belief and utterly discouraged, and just now if it were possible would gather my race in my arms and fly far away with them."[6]

Wells was beginning to learn that the power of racism was deep and wide in those classified as "white," and she would later lift up a phrase that Ronald Reagan would use as one of his hallmark phrases: "Eternal vigilance is the price of liberty." Wells meant it in the sense that we know it today: racism is deeply embedded and intertwined in our American consciousness, and we must always be working to mitigate its loathsome power.

Though some marked the Obama presidency as the death knell of the power of racism, many in the South did not. We were astonished at this turn of events that led to his election, but as native Southerners, raised in the power of white supremacy, we knew that the hold of racism remained mighty in our hearts and in our structures and institutions. The racism that undergirded slavery and neo-slavery is both resistant and resilient, and much work needs to be done to dislodge its power from our individual and collective hearts. We wished that the election of Barack Obama as president could have changed that, but we also knew that it could not and did not.

In regards to race in America, there are at least three passages that we have all traveled. The first was the European landings and settlement, when cheap labor was needed to work the land

6. Miriam Decosta-Willis, ed., *The Memphis Diary of Ida B. Wells* (Boston: Beacon Press, 1995), 140–41.

and grow the economy. Indentured servants and slaves were brought to do this work. During this time, the idea of race and slavery were married, and the idea developed that people of African descent were meant, by God and by biological destiny, to be slaves forever. This marriage was debated fiercely at the adoption of the Constitution: does the idea of "all {men} created equal" in the Declaration of Independence apply to those people held as slaves? The slaveholders won the battle at the constitutional convention, and indeed people held as slaves (and native Americans) were deemed to be 60 percent human beings.[7]

The second passage occurred at the Civil War, Reconstruction, and its aftermath. Through the dedication of many abolitionists and soldiers and the deaths of almost 700,000 in the Civil War, some progress was made to seek to establish the humanity and citizenship of those designated as "black." In a speech given in 1965, James Baldwin describes the situation, "So where we are now is that a whole country of people believe I'm a 'nigger,' and I *don't*, and the battle's on! Because if I am not what I've been told I am, then it means that *you're* not what you thought *you* were *either*. And that is the *crisis*."[8] The idea of "niggers," an idea at the heart of white supremacy, dwells deeply in the American psyche, however, and it did not take long for the slaveholders to use violence, racism, and legislation to reestablish what Doug Blackmon calls "neo-slavery."[9] By the decade of the 1890s, white supremacy was in full bloom in the South and in other places. The 1896 Supreme Court ruling in *Plessy v. Ferguson* reinforced and codified this idea that Baldwin illuminated, that we as a country believed that we needed our "n-words." Neo-slavery was firmly reestablished, and it would last until 1965.

---

7. Laurence Goldstone, *Dark Bargain* (New York: Walker and Company, 2005), 104–7.

8. James Baldwin, *Price of the Ticket* (New York: St. Martin's Press, 1985), 325–32.

9. Douglas A. Blackmon, *Slavery by Another Name* (New York: Doubleday, 2010), 402.

Fortunately for us all, there were people classified as "black" (and a few classified as "white") who were determined to fight for the idea of equality and the recognition of the humanity of black people. All through those years, there were strong voices such as Ida Wells, who fought for a different point of view, a view more closely aligned with the idea that all people are created equal. This led to the third passage, which caught fire in the 1950s, with the Supreme Court decision of *Brown v. Board of Education* in 1954, the Montgomery bus boycott of 1955–56, and the lynching of Emmett Till in 1955. These and many other actions would lead to the passage of the Civil Rights Act in 1964 and the Voting Rights Act in 1965, which offered the promise of ending neo-slavery. As before in the other two passages, white supremacy roared again. We are not sure how the transition for this third passage on race and white supremacy will end in our country.

Nibs remembers his sense of hope on a cold, dark January morning as he arrived at the Silver Springs Metro Station to get on the train about 6 a.m. In spite of the cold and early hour, there was a festive atmosphere, as more and more people boarded the train as it made stops on the way to Union Station in DC. We were celebrating a moment that we had thought we would never see—the inauguration of the first black man ever elected president of the United States. We passed through the security checkpoints near the Capitol, and then found our seats. There were over one million people in the National Mall that day, and as far as I could tell, we were all celebrating this remarkable achievement and this remarkable person.

And now, as we write this, we see the answer of white people to the Obama presidency: we are in the third year of the presidency of Donald Trump. He was elected by white people, with the majority of white people of both genders voting for him. We should not be surprised at this turn of events. With a few notable exceptions, the idea that white men are superior has been a staple of the American scene since the European beginnings. The idea that "all men are created equal" was originally intended to mean white men, but fortunately others have heard that it applies to them! Many of us were surprised that Donald Trump was elected president of the United States, yet history reminds us that whenever there is some advance toward racial or gender justice, there is a backlash and a regathering of white male power.

The election of 2020 will tell us much about our future, but for now we must seek the wisdom and justice that we can. This is a crucial time in our history, and another time of great danger, as reactionary forces seek to turn back the small tides of progress that has been made. Though it feels brand new and unique, our time bears many similarities to the years after Reconstruction, when hard-won rights for African Americans were stripped away by the resurgence of the power of white supremacy. Thus, it is fitting to turn to our elders and witnesses, as we are doing in this book.

Ida Wells was born in slavery, grew and matured during Reconstruction, and fought fiercely for the freedom that she found in the Reconstruction time. She did this while it was being stripped away in a tidal wave of racism and white supremacy. Her life and witness offer hope and possibility for us.

Though American history is rather pessimistic on this level, we choose to be inspired by Ida Wells whose life was dedicated to the idea of equity and justice for all. Her life and witness remind us of the fierceness and dedication needed to be a voice for justice, touching so many points of "intersectionality": categories such as race, gender, class that overlap one another and are in conversation—and often in tension—with one another. And we are focusing on her because her witness has been greatly undervalued in American history. In these challenging times, we must be guided by her life and witness—though she did not win as many victories as one wishes she had, she was never defeated.

CHAPTER 2

"Crusade for Justice"

The life of Ida Wells has become much better known over the past thirty years, when we first encountered her witness.[1] While we assume that readers will know a bit of her story, a review of the highlights is in order.

Ida Wells was born into slavery in Holly Springs, Mississippi, in 1862. Her father was held as a slave but also was a skilled carpenter, and her mother insisted on education for their children. When freedom came in 1865, her father, Jim Wells, was instrumental in establishing a school for African American kids in Holly Springs, and Ida would attend there. The school still is functioning today as Rust College. After the Civil War, Ida Wells grew up with a sense of possibility as Reconstruction sought to establish equity and parity for people formerly held as slaves. This happened despite all the efforts to reinstate slavery during this time.

Two major events changed the trajectory of Ida's life. In the 1876 presidential election, no candidate received a majority of the electoral votes, so it was given to a fifteen-member commission to decide who the next president would be. Though some scholars dispute the idea, it is generally agreed that even though Republican Rutherford Hayes had lost the popular vote, he won commission votes by promising to withdraw the remaining federal troops from

---

1. To learn more about Wells, see Alfreda Duster, ed., *Crusade for Justice: The Autobiography of Ida B. Wells* (Chicago: University of Chicago Press, 1970), and Paula Giddings, *Ida: A Sword Among Lions* (New York: HarperCollins, 2008).

the South. He was named president, and the withdrawal happened shortly thereafter in 1877, ending Reconstruction and leaving the white South able to fully restore its domination, now in the name of "neo-slavery."[2] This was a huge change in the South, and although it would be the 1890s before the white South was able to codify neo-slavery, Ida Wells and many others would live under its monstrous power.

The second major event for Ida Wells happened one year later in 1878. Yellow fever swept through the Mississippi River valley, and Ida was sent to stay with her grandmother in the country. While there, they received the terrible news that both Ida's father and mother had died in the epidemic. Ida headed back to Holly Springs and found that her father's Masonic brothers were dividing up her siblings so that they would have a home. Showing her characteristic determination and firepower, Ida refused to allow this to happen. She emphasized strongly that she would oversee her siblings and provide for their care. The adults reluctantly agreed, and for the rest of their childhoods, her siblings would be under her care in one form or fashion—quite an undertaking for a sixteen-year-old! She then lied about her age and got a teaching job in order to support her family.

For several years she worked and raised her siblings, meanwhile moving to Memphis, where she began to engage African Americans in the city. She rode the train to her teaching job on the outskirts of Memphis. It was on one of these trips that the incident happened where she was ordered to move to the "black" car and then thrown off the train when she refused to do so. Here we see a lesson that Ida Wells learned about the devastating power of racism. It was not just the opinions of those individuals classified as "white" that were the problem. She had encountered a dominating white man in the train conductor, but she had also

---

2. For more on this, see Goldstone, *Dark Bargain*, 104–8.

encountered a sympathetic white man in the former Union soldier who was the judge in the court, who ruled in her favor. In the decision of the Tennessee Supreme Court, Ida saw clearly that the law, i.e., the system of the order of society, was filled with racism and was now expressly designed to favor those classified as "white," despite the deaths of almost 700,000 people in the Civil War to seek to make it otherwise. In her diary entry (highlighted above in the introduction), we saw her despair both for herself and for her kin, those people classified as "black" in American culture. Her answer on that day was the image of flying away, a powerful African image of escaping the oppression of racism by taking flight.

One of Ida Wells's great gifts, however, was resistance and resilience. Though despairing and discouraged, those emotions did not paralyze her. During her days as a school teacher in the 1880s, she also began to write articles, first for her church weekly, then for local black newspapers. She found her calling! She was passionate and skilled, and she was a dedicated reporter. By 1886, her reports on black life were appearing around the country in black newspapers. In 1889, she bought a one-third interest in *Free Speech and Headlight*, a small black-owned paper in Memphis. As one of the few women reporters, she found more than her share of sexism, but she persevered, and she began to be recognized for her skills as a reporter rather than the novelty of her gender.[3]

Then came the next major event to influence her life: three of her acquaintances were lynched in Memphis in March 1892. One of them, Tom Moss, had named her as godmother to his daughter. Their crime? The three African Americans were running a successful grocery store in competition with a white-owned store across the street in a black neighborhood. The owner of the white store gathered a mob to attack their rival store, and the African

---

3. Dorothy Sterling, *Black Foremothers* (New York: Feminist Press, 1988), 73–75.

Americans returned fire when they were attacked. Three white men were wounded, but none were killed. Thirty-one African Americans were arrested, but later they were all removed from the jail by masked raiders. Three of them, including Ida Wells's good friend Tom Moss, were executed in a lynching.[4]

If she had not done so already, Wells began to connect the dots behind the motivations for this lynching and many others. She discerned that the lynchings of black people were not responses to individual crimes but rather part of a system-wide effort to reestablish white supremacy throughout the South. The charge of rape against black men as a justification for these murders now rang hollow for Wells. In response, she began a study of the 728 lynchings over the previous ten years. She used white newspapers as her primary sources, and her findings were astonishing to all: only one-third of those lynched were even charged with rape. Some were not charged at all, and other charges included assault, insolence, and theft.

She protested strongly against these lynchings and the white justifications for them. She began to write about them and their sinister purpose in her paper, *Free Speech*. In early May 1892, she published a blistering editorial about the real purpose for lynching black people, also implying that some of the liaisons between black men and white women were consensual, not rape. She was on a trip to New York, and when she arrived there, she was met by her friend and colleague T. Thomas Fortune, editor of the *New York Age*. He greeted her: "Well, we've been a long time getting you to New York, but now that you are here I am afraid that you'll have to stay." When she indicated that his comment made no sense, he showed her a copy of a New York paper, which narrated events in Memphis after her *Free Speech* editorial. Her offices had been burned to the ground, and she was threatened with being lynched

_____

4. Ibid., 78–79.

herself if she returned to Memphis.[5] She would not return to the South again until some thirty years later, in 1922.

In many ways, this was a major turning point for Ida Wells. She now determined to work against lynching and racism and for women's rights on a national and international level. She became one of the leading advocates against lynching, and she made two trips to Great Britain to develop support there for the antilynching campaign. She developed a rapport with Frederick Douglass in his later years. He indicated to her that even he, the giant of the antislavery movement, had begun to believe—just a little bit—that black men's sexuality was part of the issue in all the lynchings.[6] He was grateful to Ida Wells for reminding him that lynchings were about white supremacy, not black sexuality. He wrote an introduction to her *Southern Horrors: Lynch Law in All Its Phases*, published in 1892.

Wells was a powerful and fierce speaker on the subjects of racial justice, the need to engage and defeat white supremacy, and rights for women. In 1895, in the midst of her touring and writing, she married attorney Ferdinand Barnett and moved to Chicago. Her wedding announcement was on the front page of the *New York Times* Style section. She delayed the event three times because she was so busy speaking against lynching.[7] Once she got married, she sought to balance domestic life (including having four children) and her activist life. Others watched her balancing act, and some, like her friend Susan B. Anthony, criticized her for choosing family life over political life. Catherine will explore this relationship more fully in chapter 5.

Wells struggled with what Anthony called "divided duty" and sought to make it work on both sides. She chafed that this

---

5. Duster, *Crusade*, 61.

6. Ibid., 72.

7. Nikole Hannah-Jones, "When Ida B. Wells Married, It Was a Page One Story," *New York Times*, January 23, 2017, p. 10.

"divided duty" issue came up for women but not for men. She took her first son, Charles, with her to many meetings in his infancy, but when she had her second child, Herman, in 1897, she decided to retire from public life to tend to her family. The retirement lasted five months, when she responded to a call to advocate on behalf of justice for a postmaster lynched in South Carolina.[8] With the birth of two other children, daughters Ida and Alfreda, she slowed down in public life considerably, but she remained a tireless worker against lynchings and for racial justice.

One of the ways that she sought to address women's issues was the formation of women's clubs and national associations of women around political issues. She helped to organize the first National Conference of Colored Women in Boston in 1895, and she attended their first convention in Washington, DC, in 1896, when they changed their name to the National Association of Colored Women. This meeting was a combining of many streams: women from the antislavery days, such as Frances E. W. Harper and the powerful Harriet Tubman, joining now with those struggling against the reinstatement of neo-slavery under Jim Crow. Wells established women's clubs in Chicago and Illinois and helped to organize the women to work for equity on the local, state, and national levels.

Things were changing on the national scene, as the white supremacists in the South linked with antiblack allies in the north to reestablish "slavery by another name," as Doug Blackmon so aptly called it. The death of Frederick Douglass in 1895 left a huge vacuum in national voices for racial equality, and Booker T. Washington stepped in to fill the gap. Washington, however, seemed to prefer agitation for self-improvement for African Americans over agitation for equal rights. Washington gave a speech at the opening of Piedmont Park in Atlanta in

---

8. Sterling, *Black Foremothers*, 99.

September 1895 in which he seemed to surrender the work for racial equality to the rising tide of racism. He was astute politically and became the most powerful black man in America, but Wells and others like W. E. B. Du Bois strenuously opposed this direction. Wells put it like this in her autobiography:

> Mr. Washington's theory had been that we ought not to spend our time agitating for our rights; that we had better give attention to trying to be first-class people in a jim crow car than insisting that the jim crow car be abolished.[9]

Washington's philosophy was complicated, but in the end, it affirmed the white supremacist point of view, that people of African descent were not equal to people of Anglo descent. Those classified as "black" did not have equal rights because they were not deserving of them.

This was the mantra during slavery, and while it wobbled a bit during Reconstruction, by the 1890s it had returned in full force, not just in the South but throughout the nation. Washington read the political winds better than did Ida Wells, but his subsequent surrender of the struggles for racial equality gave white supremacy political and even scientific cover for its views. In 1896 the Supreme Court decided 8–1 in *Plessy v. Ferguson* that "separate but equal" was the law of the land. In practice it actually meant "separate and unequal." In 1898, whites in Wilmington, North Carolina, staged a coup d'etat, overthrowing the legitimately elected black city government, killing many black citizens in the process. Ida Wells appealed to President William McKinley to intercede, but he refused to do so. Wells then publicly criticized President McKinley for his allowing white supremacy to prevail. Her growing radicalism brought her into conflict with many organizations that had welcomed her earlier, both on political and sexist grounds.

---

9. Duster, *Crusade*, 265.

With four children now, Wells leaned back toward the domestic side of the "divided duty," never dropping out, but spending less time on the road and more time closer to home. In 1909 she went to New York to participate in the founding of the National Association for the Advancement of Colored People (NAACP), where she made an impassioned plea to adopt a strong antilynching platform. While she had hoped to be named as one of the forty founding committee members, her radicality kept her off the list, and she admitted in her autobiography that her hurt feelings clouded her judgment. She refused to allow her name to be amended to the list, and she left the meeting.[10]

In 1912 Woodrow Wilson was elected to be president of the United States, the first Southerner to hold the office since the Civil War. Women's groups were agitating for the right to vote for women, and they organized a march on the day before Wilson's inauguration in 1913. Wells went to DC to participate in it, but the National American Woman Suffrage Association told her that she could not join the march because they did not want to antagonize the white Southern women. Wells dropped back a few rows and joined in the march anyway, stepping in to march with the Illinois delegation. She would return to Washington later in 1913 as part of the delegation from the National Equal Rights League, founded by William Monroe Trotter of Boston. They met with President Wilson to urge him to disavow the idea of resegregation of the federal government. Wilson heard them and promised to assist them, but he did not. Indeed, segregation in the offices of the federal government was reestablished early in Wilson's presidency.

All during this time of her "divided duty," Wells formed clubs to assist those African Americans fleeing persecution in the South in the great migration. The main club was called the Negro Fellowship League, and it offered housing, meals, counseling, and

---

10. Duster, *Crusade*, 325–26.

fellowship for those migrating north. Wells not only talked about these kinds of things, but she herself put them into action. When the funding ran out for the center, she obtained a job as a probation officer and used her salary to fund the League's activities.

Because of its importance in her formation and its terroristic nature, she remained keenly interested in the continuing issue of lynching. Where the number of lynchings had diminished, they revived again during the presidency of Woodrow Wilson. She traveled to East St. Louis, Illinois, in 1917 to investigate the murders there of over forty African Americans. In 1919 another white race riot that started near Elaine, Arkansas, and spread throughout Phillips County would become the deadliest lynching in American history, when at least 237 African-Americans were murdered.[11] Its location is close to where Catherine and Nibs both grew up in Arkansas.

Twelve African American men were arrested for murder, though white marauders had clearly started the violence.[12] For the protection of the twelve, they were moved from the jail in Helena, Arkansas, to Little Rock. They had been convicted and sentenced to death, and they were given stays of execution several times, as their nationally known case, *Moore v. Dempsey*, made it to the US Supreme Court. Early in the case, Ida Wells began to raise funds for their defense, and one of the twelve wrote her and asked her to help them and to visit them. In January 1922, she decided to go to Arkansas to visit the men. It would be her first trip South since she arrived in New York in May 1892, shortly after her offices in Memphis had been firebombed, and a price put on her head.

In that light, she was somewhat anxious, and as she got closer to Helena, she went incognito as a cousin of one of the men in

---

11. Campbell Robertson, "History of Lynchings in the South Documents Nearly 4,000 Names," *New York Times*, February 10, 2015, *https://nyti.ms/1z3dYQx*.

12. For a full account of this case, see Richard Cortner, *A Mob Intent on Death* (Middletown, CT: Wesleyan University Press, 1988), and Grif Stockley, *Blood in Their Eyes* (Fayetteville: University of Arkansas Press, 2004).

jail. She and a group of the men's relatives went to visit the men in jail, and the men's eyes lit up when they were told that the visitor was not a cousin but was Ida B. Wells. They talked for a long while, and Wells took many notes on their stories. Then the men sang some songs of their own and some spirituals. At the end of the singing, Ida Wells gave them a charge:

> I have been listening to you for nearly two hours. You have talked and sung and prayed about dying, and forgiving your enemies, and of feeling sure that you are going to be received in the New Jerusalem because your God knows that you are innocent of the offense for which you expect to be electrocuted. But why don't you pray to live and ask to be freed? The God you serve is the God of Paul and Silas who opened their prison gates, and if you have all the faith you say you have, you ought to believe that he will open your prison doors too. . . . Quit talking about dying; if you believe your God is all powerful, believe that he is powerful enough to open these prison doors, and say so.[13]

As in so many cases, Ida Wells proved to be prophetic. *Moore vs. Dempsey* was the first case in the twentieth century to be considered by the Supreme Court in regard to the rights of African Americans in the South in criminal matters. The Court heard the case in January 1923, and in February ruled 6–2 that the twelve had been denied their constitutional rights. The case was remanded back to the lower courts, and eventually all twelve were freed. Wells noted that their Arkansas attorney Scipio Jones gave her credit for increasing publicity about the case and helping to raise so much money. Later one of the twelve who were freed showed up at her home in Chicago to thank her for her efforts.[14] It was one of the

---

13. Duster, *Crusade*, 402–3.

14. Ibid., 403–4.

few cases where Ida Wells was part of the winning side on the issue of racial justice, yet she remained a strong voice and activist for racial justice in the midst of the tidal wave of racism. White supremacy swept over the South and indeed the entire country.

Ida Wells was a mighty voice for justice for African Americans, for women, and for those who were poor. Her life is a testimony and a witness for all of us as we consider our place in this current atmosphere of danger and fear. Her times, even more than our own, saw the forces of violence and oppression and white supremacy regather strength, just as they are doing in our day. The final chapter of her autobiography is entitled "The Price of Liberty." She never finished the chapter because she was struck with a sudden illness and died in just a few days in March 1931. This is the paragraph that began that final chapter:

> Eternal vigilance is the price of liberty, and it does seem to me that notwithstanding all these social agencies and activities there is not that vigilance which should be exercised in the preservation of our rights. This leads me to wonder if we are not too well satisfied to be able to point to our wonderful institutions with complacence and draw the salaries connected therewith, instead of being alert as the watchman on the wall.[15]

Questions for Further Reflection

1. Which parts of this chapter make you want to learn more about Ida Wells?
2. What puzzles you about the narrative of the life of Ida Wells?
3. How have things changed in terms of racial justice since Ida Wells was alive? What has not changed?

---

15. Ibid., 415.

CHAPTER 3

"To Tell the Truth Freely"

Nearly twenty years ago, leading a class on Ida B. Wells at Wesleyan College in Macon, Georgia, Catherine's students surprised her by noting that Wells reminded them of her. This chapter is a comparative reflection from Catherine.

I begin by acknowledging that there was little in my early life designed to help me believe that I could tell the truth either freely or otherwise. My early life, as a little African American girl in rural Arkansas, taught me to be quiet. The primary lessons came from living with my illiterate sharecropping father, who suffered from post-traumatic stress disorder, and my mother, who graduated from college the year that I turned eighteen. My father's condition was caused by the premature death of my twelve-year-old brother who died because he was black and poor and could not get medical care from the local hospital.

Though my brother had died before I was born, I heard my father talk about him almost every day. He told us many times how the local hospital had informed him that he should take my brother, Garland, to the charity hospital in Shreveport, Louisiana, which was seventy-five miles from our home since my parents did not have money and the hospital did not treat African Americans anyway. By the time my father managed to obtain transportation for them, Garland was far too sick to be saved. He died in the hospital at age twelve.

There was more stress and distress in our household than was good for any of us. I did not understand what caused it until years later when I began to realize how my father's experience as a disempowered illiterate black man in America framed his life. During my early years I thought that he was simply difficult to live with and I had to find a way to escape.

So at the early age of eight I began to practice ways to cope. One of the ways was to rise early before almost everyone in my family and go out to sit on the backdoor steps and watch the world wake up as the sun rose. There were times when I was puzzled about what motivated me to do this, but I am aware now that my effort to find ways to cope with a household that made me feel that escape was necessary helped me to form that habit. In addition to that, I believe that there was a deep inquiring mind and spirit in my eight-year-old body that was being nurtured onto a lifetime path of inquiring about the way to liberation. As an adult, I wonder what gave me this trait and my best analysis tells me that it was simply grace that prodded me and helped me to learn to cope in a world that would be difficult for many years to come.

Perhaps it is my inquiring mind and willingness to be different that put me on the path that would cross the one that Ida B. Wells was traveling. Though I did not meet her until I was in my early forties and she was born eighty-four years earlier than I was, there is so much that we share, and as I continue to live, the common threads become even more apparent to me. My soul resonates with her and the ways in which she chose to stand in the world.

Unlike Wells, I did not lose both of my parents, though I lost my father when I was sixteen. My mother was present and was gainfully employed, but still I assumed a great amount of responsibility in our household and felt that I had to help my mother as much as possible. This sense of responsibility led me to seek employment as a youngster, but the jobs never paid more than $3.00 per day. My jobs were cleaning houses for white women, babysitting, and working in a hotel as a short order cook in the hotel kitchen.

Though I was not compelled as Wells had been at sixteen to lie about my age so I could get a job in order to take care of younger siblings, the small amounts of money that I made did help my mother to make ends meet as she worked to take care of the four of us on a meager Arkansas teacher's salary. My mother's resourcefulness helped me to learn the meaning of "making a way out of no way."

Clearly, just like Wells, I learned a great deal from my parents, although it would be years before I would come to see that fact and to appreciate it. Just as Wells had learned to be independent from her father and to have a deep and abiding faith from her devout mother, I learned from mine. My mother taught me that education was one of the most valuable possessions I could ever gain. Daddy taught me to love the land. Though he was a sharecropper, he loved the land and would rise even before me and go out to walk all around the field to see what had happened to the crops during the night. His love for the land was instructive to me, helping me to understand the need to be grounded as I traveled through the landmine of segregation and other forces of oppression that were not poised in my favor.

I share with Wells an inner motivation that propels me forward to this day. Wells recalled that she does not know when she began to read; the process must have begun very early in her life. She left school at sixteen to go to work, yet she maintained her curious mind and the courage to follow it throughout her life as she fought against lynching, racism, women's oppression, and poverty. The archetypal spirit of resistor grew in both of us as we walked along the paths presented to us. Of course, the walk was different because she was traveling in the nineteenth and twentieth centuries and I in the twentieth and twenty-first, but the

African descent when there was a crisis created on our campus by a grave act of injustice.

The act was the killing of a fifteen-year-old boy from our neighborhood by the campus security guard. It was murder and the person who did it was not held accountable. Our campus was filled with great turmoil around the injustice of the matter and the way in which the college worked to return to a sense of normalcy as quickly as possible. It was amid this turmoil that I caught a glimpse of their authentic and deep desire to do what was right for us as students of African descent, which I had never seen expressed by a white person at any time before. It was their honesty and willingness to risk their place in the white world for what they believed to be right for us that opened my eyes to the possibility of a relationship with a white person.

The door of my heart opened and allowed them to enter. It was the first time that I took the chance on letting a white person into the sacred space of my heart and it had been made possible because of their open hearts. Those relationships have lasted for over fifty years and helped me to be able to move along the path that my life needed to take me in my work of resistance to oppression and the pursuit of liberation.

Although I did not discover Wells until much later in my life, I think that my soul was always searching for her kindred spirit as a sister of resistance. When I left Brinkley, Arkansas, I was eighteen years old and had only been to Memphis, Tennessee, to visit the zoo and to Louisiana because one of my older sisters lived there. My older brothers lived in California and I began daydreaming about going to college there in my teenage years. At eighteen, I boarded a Greyhound bus and headed to Compton, California. I made the declaration that I was leaving the South with no plans to ever return in this lifetime.

Unlike Wells, I had the opportunity to leave the South because I chose to do so; she left because of threats to her life.

Through her writing she made whites so angry that they burned down her newspaper office in Memphis and placed a bounty on her head. Yet despite this, she would come back to the South because she was more concerned about being true to herself than choosing the safe path. The realization of a similar spirit in myself was quite surprising.

This spirit had accompanied me along my path for longer than I knew, but the circumstances of my life allowed it to be mostly dormant. It was not until I went to college that I was given the opportunity to take a stand for justice in situations that would be challenging on many levels. My learned habit of keeping silent was challenged by the struggles for liberation that I had to navigate as a young African American woman in college.

As I was being asked to fight for the liberty of myself and for others, some of those challenges came too early in my life because I was not sure about my identity as a person. It was a terrifying experience. I wish that I had known Ida B. Wells before I had to navigate my way through some of those times.

Wells models what it means to have an authentic self. I have always longed to be an authentic person. Though I did not begin to articulate the "Who am I?" query until I was in college, the question was being asked at some level in my heart many years before. In the early years of her life, Wells seemed to ponder that question quite vigorously as she worked her way through the challenges of relationships with men and other women. She struggled with money in those early years as well. While it is tempting when reading her to simply resist her lament about all her struggles, especially those around money and buying things, my sense of honesty leads me to look at my own struggles and to take her seriously. She is described as "sometimes sick or cold, paying bills, mounting debts, fighting slander and fighting internal demons—a quick temper and sharp tongue—that bring on occasional bouts of loneliness and feelings of alienation from others."

She describes herself at those times as "just drifting along."[1] She is wounded by some of the things that are said about her by a few young men who accuse her of high-handedness in her courtships, and she says of them, "[They] have formed themselves in a league against a defenseless girl." She goes on to speak about her financial hardship again, "[M]y system is not in good order and I cannot consult a physician till I get some money. If I once get out of debt I hope that this lesson will be remembered and profited by: to think I am in debt more than one month's salary and if anything should happen I have not enough money coming to me to cancel my expenses."[2] This struggle with finances and the attitudes of some men resonates with my experience as well.

I believe that there is great value in being able to learn from the struggles of a giant warrior woman such as Wells and to spend time reflecting upon the ways in which one's life can intersect with such a person. This type of reflection can be helpful in terms of providing encouragement for staying faithful to the call to resist oppression and to help relieve the projection of perfection that often blinds us to the reality of the heroine's humanity.

Thus, reading Wells's *Memphis Diary* and hearing of some of the conflicts that she had with men who did not seem to understand the type of person that she was and who did not seem to be worthy of her true affection is affirming. I share this life experience with her.

Boys did not like me because I was usually excelling in school, running for an office that no girl had stood for before or staying to myself so that I did not have to talk to them. While this was true in high school, it did not change much in college. There were a handful of men that I found attractive at a distance, but scrutiny always left me wondering what I saw in them in the first

---

1. Miriam Decosta-Willis, *The Memphis Diary of Ida B. Wells* (Boston: Beacon Press, 1995), 20.

2. Ibid., 33.

place. In addition to that, most of them were never interested in the things that I found to be crucial.

Wells's shopping habits were not exactly like mine, though I never had enough money, I tended simply to do without things because there was no way to obtain them and I did not have any sources of credit. Survival was always uppermost in my mind, though that same kind of energy that pushed me to resist the segregated waiting room and to rise before sunrise pushed me forward.

When I think about that era in my life and read about a similar time for Wells, I am reminded of this comment from Nobel Prize–winning author Toni Morrison. She said, "[The black woman] had nothing to fall back on; not maleness, not whiteness, not ladyhood, not anything. And out of the profound desolation of her reality, she may very well have invented herself."[3] In the circle of psychology, this process of self-invention would mostly likely be described as individuation. It is the process of separating oneself from others and becoming who you are going to be in the world. Wells did this by forging a path that was different than most other young women in her age group. She was independent, working, taking care of siblings, moving into activism, speaking up about things such as lynching and women's rights when others were choosing silence.

My effort at self-invention began as I boarded a Greyhound bus for California at age eighteen to go to college. I had a solid internal core that was pointed toward self-invention and liberation even though I did not know it. I was not sure what I was going to do and how I was going to become the person that I was put on the earth to become. But it is only in rare cases where anyone sees the bigger picture of their life. Generally, it is in the process of reflection that the path begins to become clarified. So, in Wells's

---

3. Toni Morrison, "What the Black Woman Thinks of Women's Lib," *New York Times*, August 22, 1971, *https://www.nytimes.com/1971/08/22/archives/what-the-black-woman-thinks-about-womens-lib-the-black-woman-and.html*.

case, she simply kept putting one foot in front of the other. She kept standing up for what was right. She kept speaking out and she kept writing. She was honest about her longings for stability and an easier life, but she stayed faithful to her life as it unfolded.

It was her faithfulness that made her someone that history cannot erase. Of course, she had no clues about what her legacy would be in those early years when she was in the process of becoming the authentic person that she was put on the earth to become. She simply kept moving forward. This path is so familiar to me because I did not know that I would answer justice's call and stand up to oppressors as I moved through my life as a student and later as a more mature adult. I had no idea that each time I resisted that I would be called to resist again and that I would do it. I did not know that getting deeper into my faith journey would be a call to more resistance. No one told me what I was getting into and I did not really have any markers to show me the way that the path would unfold.

Clearly the resisting was not as dangerous for me as it was for Wells when our lives are reflected upon, but when one is living out their call, there is no way to make such comparisons and they are not always helpful. This is true simply because when the unchartered path is being followed, it does not seem safe and it is never clear what the outcome might be. While Wells knew that the white folks who put a bounty on her head would be happy to see her dead, she had no way to know whether she would be kept safe.

I remember when that child was killed on our campus, an army of police were called out to handle us, the student protestors. We knew that they could kill us, but we had no way to know whether they would. For some reason we were not killed, just as Wells was not killed. All of us had some reason to be left on this earth and we had no clue what it was on the days that our lives were spared. But it did not matter because we had said yes at the deep core of ourselves and there was no turning back.

Wells did not return to Memphis after learning that her office had been burned. I left Los Angeles after being confronted by police in the last place I had ever expected to see a police officer: on my college campus while marching for justice for a fifteen-year-old boy who was murdered. I moved to Georgia of all places. It surprised me that I wanted to go back to the South, the place that I had left eight years earlier vowing never to return.

It is easy to understand that Wells needed to move away from the South after having her newspaper office burned down and having large bounties placed on her head. It is harder to understand why she would ever come back, and as I reflect upon that question, I must think about why I came back myself.

The answer for me is complex. A portion of the answer lies in the fact that after reading *Julian Bond, Black Rebel: A Biography*[4] and the assessment about the new South, I thought that it was a good place to which to return. But beyond that, I think that my soul needed to be in this place that has been dubbed "America's Holy Land"[5] by Bishop Robert Wright, who describes it as follows, "I took my family to the Holy Land some time ago . . . you ever been? . . . You know the Holy Land . . . Alabama, Mississippi, Tennessee . . . Georgia. . . . I don't remember the first time I said it, the thing about the American South being the Holy Land. It came from somewhere beyond my head up to my mouth, but I am sure it was before the trip."[6] The trip that had been taken by the bishop, his wife, and four little children was to Selma, Montgomery, Birmingham, Lookout Mountain, and other sites and caused him to say upon their return, "Back

---

4. John Neary, *Julian Bond, Black Rebel: A Biography* (New York: William Morrow & Co, 1971).

5. Robert Wright, "The American South Is Our Holy Land," in *Living Into God's Dream: Dismantling Racism In America*, ed. Catherine Meeks (New York: Morehouse Publishing, 2016), 119.

6. Ibid.

home . . . Beth and I resumed our hectic lives. But, we had seen something. Been somewhere special. Not the special you feel from seeing important artifacts. But the special you feel when you see an old family photo album of relatives you never knew. Special like discovering your ancestry."[7] In an effort to create a better understanding of Holy Land, Wright goes on to say, "Maybe the traditional understanding of the phrase Holy Land can better shed some light on what I am trying to convey. . . . The land is geo-theological—holy geology and geography—which is the location where both the personal and communal experience of God in past days occurred. The place where significance and guidance for present-day actions abound, in addition to the sense of promise of continued relationship, identity, and even prosperity in the future with God. . . . The land is holy because labor and pain, joy and grief, birth and death, war and peace, prayer to and betrayal of God have happened on the land and therefore set it apart. It knows and is deeply known."[8]

In some ways the call back to the South came from "somewhere beyond my head," from the deep recesses of my soul and I cannot help wondering if the same was true for Wells. She too came and went in the South despite the danger. She came to visit victims falsely accused and waiting in a Helena, Arkansas, jail to see what their final plight would be, though it was a risk for her. The call was louder than the voice of fear and she listened to the call as I have done.

My mother was worried when I left Los Angeles in my old 1980s Plymouth Valiant, which was not in good enough shape to drive from California to Georgia, but I was young and brave enough to think that it would make the trip. It was only the grace of God that got me to Georgia in that old car that burned far too

---

7. Ibid., 121.

8. Ibid.,122.

many quarts of oil and would often overheat. I made it to Atlanta and drove it for several more months until it finally died sitting in front of my apartment. When I think of that old car and its life span, it reminds me to sing "Amazing Grace."

It took a few years to realize that there was a reason for me to be back in the South and that I was in Georgia to do something more than just struggle to survive. My sense of purpose was not clear to me for a good while and neither was it for Wells in her early life. I identify deeply with that part of her struggle in those early years when she was trying to hear what path she was called to follow. But there was never any question in my mind nor Ida B. Wells's that we had work to do that was larger than merely having a job.

My journey took me on a winding road through working in prison education, a mental health clinic, going to graduate school, college and university work, and multiple layers of community activism around health, education, crime and violence prevention, race relations, and child welfare issues. I learned a lot about working in the race relations arena about white people who helped to form various entities that were supposedly designed to dismantle racism but turned out to be mostly designed to make sure that nothing radical happened. I worked with a group in Macon, Georgia, that met for more than a year in attempt to determine what its mission was going to be, but after deciding the mission and opening an office, it became clear that the group of white businessmen and women along with the black participants were looking for a safe route to change. Since there is no safe route to significant change around dismantling racism, I resigned. It was very frustrating to work with that group because they were quite articulate in their defense of gradualism and obstructing any project that might have led to substantial systemic change.

Racial healing is one of the issues where I have made the most significant connections with Ida B. Wells around lynching and understanding how owning that history relates to building new foundations so racial healing can take place. Though she was a pioneer in several arenas, her work against lynching was phenomenal. It was that work that angered the white population the most because she refused to allow the white narrative that blamed lynching on the behavior of black people, especially the men, to stand as the truth. The age-old story of the depravity of the black man being the reason that white men had to lynch them to maintain safety was a lie and Wells never failed to make that fact crystal clear. She laid the responsibility of the indefensible act of lynching at the feet of the white perpetrators where it belonged. She observed that "in fact, for all kinds of offenses and, for no offenses—from murders to misdemeanors, men and women are put to death without judge or jury; so that, although the political excuse was no longer necessary, the wholesale murder of human beings went on just the same."[9] Thus it was quite clear that one's behavior did not have much to do with whether one fell victim to lynching. Though Wells worked tirelessly to end lynching, America managed to create an unbelievable legacy of massive lynching and grave moral injury to the nation's psyche for many years through this brutal practice.

Though my work around this issue is not nearly as dangerous as it was for Wells, it has not been without challenges. The work that I have engaged in doing is dedicated to remembering those who were lynched in Georgia. From 2016 to 2018 I led the Episcopal Diocese of Atlanta in the Calling Their Names: Remembering Georgia's Lynched initiative. In 2015, approximately two hundred persons gathered at the Douglass Theater in Macon, Georgia, to participate in a memorial service and unveiling of a small marker that was placed near the front entrance to the

---

9. Ida B. Wells, *The Light of Truth*, ed. Mia Bay and Henry Louis Gates (New York: Penguin Books, 2014), 397.

theater bearing the names of seventeen people who were lynched in the Central Georgia area. The marker also indicates that there were those who were unknown.

The same type of program was held in Athens, Georgia, in 2017 at the Chestnut Grove Baptist Church and the marker was placed at the Chestnut Grove School, which is a restored one-room school house that was built in 1887 for African American children in that area. The school is on the historical registry and it is quite appropriate to have the marker with the fifty-six names of folks who were lynched in that area listed along with a note of remembrance for the ones who are unknown. In 2018, a five-foot-tall granite marker with four bronze plates with the names of all 684 persons who were lynched in Georgia and an acknowledgment of those who are unknown was placed at the Absalom Jones Center for Racial Healing.

The work of remembering the lynched has not always received great acceptance. There are those who feel that it should not be done, but I am very clear that this work is essential to the process of achieving any long-term healing and ultimately to the work of truly dismantling the racist structures that seem to be indestructible. A major portion of the work that I have done is designed to lead the participants in it to pay attention to the intersection of slavery, lynching, the prison industrial complex, the death penalty, and twenty-first-century police extrajudicial killings, which are modern-day lynchings.

The placing of markers and creating spaces for remembering along with creating material to help in exploring the intersections listed above helps to address the issue of the moral injury that lynching brought to the nation and can open a door to healing that will not be opened until deep and true healing work is embraced. Wells's unflinching courage in the face of death threats, burned down office space, and the lack of support from any type of law enforcement community stands as a striking witness to me. The amazing spirit that she brought to the work helps me to embrace the naysayers with a smile and to reaffirm my commitment to keep lynching on the forefront of the racial healing work that I lead because it is a critical part of the equation if there is to be genuine healing. As I see it, racial healing must be supported by the truth. Lynching was an amazingly horrible act of violence and degradation against African Americans and anyone that white people deemed to be a threat to the supremacy paradigm. It happened and the injury resulting from it was not simply to African Americans. There is no way that a group of people can, with a celebratory spirit, engage in such violence against another group deemed unworthy and still escape deep moral injury. Thus, all of us must be healed and the first step is in fully acknowledging what happened in the past and how it continues to inform the present. Once that is done in a sincere manner, the space can be created for healing to occur. Wells knew that the truth was a core principle in making the world a better place and I know that also. Of course, there are still acts of violence being carried out against blacks and others that must be stopped. We must acknowledge the violence of the past and seek forgiveness from our sisters and brothers who were its victims.

While the work around lynching is very liberating, it is also gut wrenching. I was caught a bit by surprise regarding the emotional impact of this work upon me. When I was preparing for the first event in Macon, I had worked on the list of the seventeen persons who were going to be placed on the marker without giving my reaction too much attention. I left my house and traveled to the grocery store and I was thinking about the work that I had just finished, and I found myself going around in circles, unable to focus. Finally, I realized that I was very close to tears and it was important to simply get out of the store and go sit in quietness for a while. As I sat in my car and cried, it became clear to me that I was simply grieving for the folks with whom I had been working over the past months and absorbing their stories. The horrors were not to be taken lightly—which I had no intention of doing—but I had not factored in how much I would need to allow the grief and rage to present itself to me and to honor it as I was trying to honor those who had been so dishonored.

No wonder there were folks who were telling me that I should not bring up this topic. I had some sense of the way in which this work would require us all to look deep into ourselves and our culture before I began, but once I was into the work, it went much deeper than I had imagined. However, I do not have a single regret about embracing the work around lynching and will continue as I described earlier in this chapter. I will continue with joy and I will do everything that I can to inspire, encourage, and support others across the United States who dare to take it on in their regions.

On the wall in my office is a picture of Ida B. Wells. There is also a framed photograph of her on my bedroom wall. She is among my cloud of witnesses and I need to see her every day to be reminded that my days will never be as challenging as hers were during the time that she lived. I have an abundance of educational, spiritual, and material resources, and even though she had resources, there was an abundance of hardship and socially sanctioned constraints to go with them.

The greatest gift that Wells brings to my life and to any others who will embrace her life and work is freedom from fear. In the beginning of this chapter, I reflected on the fact that I was not raised to think that I could have a voice. My household and the culture around me embodied an energy that led to silencing. But the desire to speak was embedded in my heart in a very deep way and though it took years for that desire to blossom in a full and complete way, it was destined to do so. Unlike me, Wells lived in a household that taught her to speak and to believe in her innate power. She was supported by her family in ways that made the segregated and oppressive forces external to her ineffective.

This is a profound point to ponder. The plague of the twenty-first century is fear. Of course, there are many of us who live each day as best we can as resistors to it, but the fear hill is steep, and many are slipping down it instead of scaling it. The twenty-four-hour news cycle is a major contributor to the fear force as well as social media and everyday life with its ups and downs. While the news and social media are good things to have, we have allowed them to become a negative force. When human beings allow themselves to be impacted by entities that are external to them in ways that prevent them from being who they were put on earth to be, it is sad.

The struggle against the darkness created by white supremacy and its child, white privilege, is one to be engaged by whites and blacks as well as all other people of color. Clearly there are powers to be engaged and that engagement takes courage. The kind of courage that Wells exhibited when she took on caretaking for her siblings at age sixteen when her parents died or when she fought the Chesapeake Railroad or when she returned to the South to engage in her liberation work even though she knew that there were white folks who would have killed her if given the chance—this is the kind of courage that must engage the powers, principalities, and spiritual wickedness that the Holy Scripture speaks about in Ephesians 6. I have pondered this passage for many years and it is clearer than ever to me how those powers are manifesting themselves in the current moment. They are supporting our collective fear and distracting too many of us from doing the work of racial healing and liberation.

Wells would have a stern rebuke for our current moment. She knew that it was more important to die standing up and being in the struggle than to be down in the ditch trying to find refuge where none existed. It would be difficult for her to understand the source of our lack of agency in so many cases today. Even though she struggled with livelihood issues and many others in early life, she managed to navigate her way through them and to emerge with a sense of agency and an understanding of the call that was hers to follow.

I am thankful to have been able to do that as well. I know others that have done so also, Nibs for one, including many of you who are reading this book. There are many others who want to join the courage caravan as well and believing that gives me hope. But across the nation there is too much fear, and it must be named and resisted. During my college years as we responded to the call to fight for liberation, we would declare that the college could have our scholarship. This was our declaration because we thought that was the worst thing that could happen to us. I am not sure that we thought as much about dying as we did our scholarships. College was important, and some of us knew that without our financial aid and scholarships, we could not have remained, so we focused upon that factor and concluded that liberation from racial oppression was more important than the scholarship. And though we did not say it, we were prepared to die.

Perhaps one of the most profound questions to be asked and answered in today's moment of struggle is, for what are you prepared to die? Though the death might not be physical, there will be some death required if we are working to help dismantle all forms of oppression both internally and externally. The idea of a new world with equity and no oppression is a bit unsettling because we have never really known liberation in its fullest. But we must begin to imagine that world of freedom for everyone if it is ever to become a reality.

Wells imagined that the world could be better than it was, and she believed that she had a right to live in that world. I believe that the world can be better than it is and that it was never God's intention for us to make the world that we have. Thus, the call from God is and always will be to create Beloved Community. A world where all of God's children, which includes every soul on the planet, can be who they were sent to the earth to become without having to be held hostage by enslaving and dehumanizing supremacists' notions that imprison the body and the soul of far too many.

Careful reading of Wells will help to deconstruct the current fear-based systems that serve the powers, principalities, and spiritual wickedness in high places which stand in the path that leads to Beloved Community. She helps us to know that they cannot have the last word unless we allow them to do so. She encourages us to heed the call and to search for the inner voice that keeps telling us that nothing but true liberation is good enough for God's children.

In addition, one can embark upon an inner journey pilgrimage to assist in conquering fear. It is helpful to do careful self-interrogation work that helps to clarify where our personal loyalties lie. Competing loyalties will thwart the work of courage building. It is important to note that courage can grow and that it does grow each time that we choose it over expediency.

Engaging in honest and clear self-interrogation work is needed to determine what your heart's desire really is around issues of liberation and justice and what you are willing to do to achieve that desire. It is quite clear to me that none of us can achieve anything of substantial substance unless our hearts are in it and helping to provide the energy that is needed to sustain the project.

It is helpful to set aside a bit of time each day to reflect upon the nature of the path that we are traveling and the reasons that we are on that path. There are times when that is not as clear as others, but at some point, there should be a glimpse of why our journey is as it is. It is helpful to keep a journal and to note thoughts and feelings. It is especially important to explore resistance and to listen to its story and, when necessary, to gather new facts for the story. The narratives that we live by can benefit from good editing when we begin to see a bigger and more illumined snapshot of our journey.

I have found the practice of silence to be very helpful in the process of creating a new narrative for myself. The old stories are often laced in fear and need to be reviewed with the new energy that comes from seeing a better picture. It is helpful to engage with a supportive community and name your own cloud of witnesses when one is trying to overcome fear.

As I have traveled on the courage-seeking pilgrimage, I have found it most helpful to seek out poets and music to help in enlarging the space in my head and heart so that there is room for the new energy of courage. It is also critical to remember that this is a journey and that while there will be small and sometimes large successes along the way, it will take a full lifetime. So it makes sense to enjoy the traveling and take each day as it is presented.

Holding on to God's unchanging hand is the most important piece of all the courage-building work and to stay open to the grace that undergirds all of the effort and fills the shallow places in our hearts and minds as we do liberation work. Grace does incomprehensible work each day to make up the deficits that are created by our limitations of energy, love, faith, hope, and will. We can be thankful for grace and the way in which God deploys it.

The journey is long, and we are far from home now, but there is a light shining at the end of the tunnel. We can catch a glimpse of that light every time we choose to embrace courage rather than fear. This realization has been one of the best sources of hope and empowerment for me. It helps me to live in a brave space where the truth can be told. It helps me to tell the truth freely and I am encouraged every day by my dear sister, Ida B. Wells.

Questions for Further Reflection

1. In order to tell the truth freely, people have to believe that there are brave spaces that will allow their truth to be heard. Where do you find such brave spaces where you can tell the truth as you see it?

2. Did you grow up in a household where you were encouraged to speak your mind or not? Do you seek out others who seem to know what they think and who are willing to speak about it when it comes to race?

3. How do you respond to the ways in which Wells embraced her life challenges?

4. What is the hardest part of this chapter for you to reflect upon?

CHAPTER 4

"My Name Is Legion"

In this chapter Nibs seeks to address the demonic power of racism in his life and in the life of our nation, and why it remains so daunting and so resistant to change. "Demonic" is used here in the biblical sense of the word: a power that takes over our identities and causes us to think and act in ways that are contrary to our own welfare and to the welfare of others.

The life and witness of Ida Wells helps us to understand the continuing depths of racism and sexism in the lives of those classified as "black" or "white." Wells took responsibility for her siblings at age sixteen. She stood up (or, more accurately, "sat down") for equality in accommodations. She raged at the unjust killing of Tom Moss and his friends. She was a strong, investigative reporter on lynchings and many other matters of racial justice. She worked hard for rights for women, including voting rights and forming social clubs. She took on black patriarchy. She helped black immigrants from the South in their adjustments to life in Chicago and elsewhere. She was a tireless champion for human rights, all the while being married and raising four children. Yet, for all her efforts, very little progress was made on human rights for people of African descent. Her spirit is an important witness—she never won many victories, but she never was defeated. Her life and her witness push us to understand the demonic powers of racism and sexism even more in the continuation of her work against them.

Luke 8:26–39 has a powerful story about demonic possession: Jesus gets off a boat in Gerasa, and a wild man steps out of the graveyard and hollers at Jesus: "What have you to do with me, Jesus, Son of the Most High God? I beg you, do not torment me!" Jesus had apparently commanded the demon to come out of the man. Then Jesus asks the man his name, and the man says "Legion." The author of Luke tells us that it means that many demons had entered the man, so many that the man had lost his identity. When Jesus asked him for his name, he did not say "Paul" or "James" or "Stephen," but "Legion."

In this seemingly weird world of demonic possession, the demons beg Jesus not to send them into the abyss, so he sends them into a herd of pigs nearby. The pigs are driven off the hill into the lake and are drowned. But the man is healed. When the townspeople come out to see what has happened, what impresses them is not the man who was healed but rather all those dead pigs in the water. They are not celebrating the healing of this brother—"Thank you, Jesus!" No, they are filled with fear—it is too costly, it is too harsh a blow to the economy. So they tell Jesus to leave—don't mess with our economy.

This is a multilayered, complex, and profound story, and for a long time, I did not know what to do with it. Thanks to Walter Wink, Gayraud Wilmore, Letty Russell, and others, I began to understand the power and reality of demonic possession in our kind of world.[1] The demons that I have to worry about are not the personal kind mentioned in this story, but this story does point us to the reality of demonic powers in the modern world. The ones that trouble me and possess me are the potent ones like

---

1. See Walter Wink, *Engaging the Powers* (Minneapolis: Augsburg Fortress Press, 1992); Gayraud Wilmore, *Black Religion and Black Radicalism* (Maryknoll, NY: Orbis Books, 1991); Letty Russell, *Household of Freedom* (Philadelphia: Westminster Press, 1989).

racism and sexism and militarism and materialism, the kind that I know in my life and in the life of others. I became demonically possessed by racism growing up, and its power is so great in me that it still pops up, and when I am asked my name, I often give its name rather than my own. And often when Jesus comes to heal me, to liberate me from my demonic possession, I join the townspeople in fear and tell him to get out of here—leave me alone with my systems!

Whatever one thinks about the literal truth of this story in Luke, its most potent meaning is its pointing us to understand our individual and communal captivity to demonic possession. But, thank God, Jesus is coming for us, coming to offer us freedom from our captivity. It will be difficult; it will be costly. We may even tell Jesus: "Get outta here!" But the great and disturbing news of this story is that Jesus Christ is coming for us—to heal us, to help us find our true identity as children of God. It's the biblical Jesus. Ida Wells knew that biblical Jesus, and she sought to follow his teachings, including the engagement with demonic powers. She is a wizard who shows us the way.

This demonic power of race definitely seeped into my soul in the 1940s and 1950s, as I grew up as a child of the segregated South on the Arkansas side of the Mississippi River. I grew up in what Doug Blackmon called "neo-slavery." Though slavery had been officially banished (except in prison—a significant and disturbing part of the Thirteenth Amendment), it was alive and well in the white South in my childhood and adolescence. It was called something else—generally "Jim Crow," but I prefer the connection to slavery that is found in the name "neo-slavery." Though its political power was evident, just as important was its psychological and theological power. I was so captured by this system that I could not imagine that African Americans were human beings like me. Segregation was viable not only because of naked political and military power—it was viable also because the hearts and imaginations of most white people had learned and come to believe that it was God's will. Woven through this was the idea that the only work of the white Christ was to get me into heaven when I died. I went to a white, segregated Presbyterian church every Sunday, and I never heard about or even dreamed about the black Jesus, a Jesus who might be interested in this world, a Jesus who might be asking me to engage the God of the Jewish prophetic tradition, a Jesus for whom the domination of the American system of slavery and the idea of whiteness itself was an abomination.

It is essential that I make clear here what is often misunderstood when we Americans, especially those of us who are classified as "white," talk about race relations or even racial justice. I was taught the racism that undergirds whiteness not by mean and devious people, although there seemed to be plenty of them immersed in this system. I was taught this system by good white people, people who supported me and loved me, people who taught me and indeed embodied to me the love of God, even if that God was white. This fact does not deny or negate the evil of the system of race, but it does point to the complications of efforts to eradicate it. The bad news is that this system of the white Christ is deeply imbedded in all of our consciousness, and it will take much work and grace to begin to move out of its captivity. It is not just a matter of the will—it involves the imagination also. The good news is that the God we know in the black Jesus is not confined to our systems, and God's love and power is calling us all out of captivity into liberation.

I grew up in Helena, Arkansas, a farming town on the Mississippi River, a town much more like the Mississippi Delta than the other parts of Arkansas, a town not far from where Catherine grew up. I cannot remember a time when I did not know race. My grandfather's grandfather owned people. I do not know if he saw them as people, but I do know that he saw them as slaves.

I have heard family stories of the people held as slaves taking the family horses down to the bottom lands to hide them from the Yankee soldiers coming through my family's home county of Marshall County, Mississippi. As far as I can tell, my familial ancestors were decent people. They were not the stereotypes of racists, lynching black people or terrorizing the countryside in white sheets at night. They loved the earth; they loved one another; they offered hospitality to white strangers; and they had a good sense of humor.

And they were racists. As far as I know, they were not night riders, but they supported that system and benefitted from it. As I write this, it sounds harsh. It is difficult for me to write, even at this moment. It is difficult because I have been taught, and I have believed that personal virtues were different from public virtues. My grandfather, my mother's father, with his great belly laugh and overly generous heart, my grandfather who cuddled me and told me that I was his favorite—my grandfather was a racist. It is difficult that such a loving and kind man was a racist, and yet, it is true.

It is this juxtaposition of being a decent individual and yet participating and supporting evils like racism that is important to keep before us. If we lose sight of this juxtaposition or deny it, we miss one of the central dynamics of the system of race. Often we deny that racism exists in white people by believing that the only racists are the brutish louts who seem to enjoy stomping and crushing people. It is deeper and much more complex than that—it is personal and individual and cultural and structural and institutional. I know this because I have it in my DNA, in my family history, and in my own consciousness. I was taught, and I came to believe, that nonwhite people, especially those classified as "black," were not human beings like me. To call a black person the "N-word" was not a pejorative usage. From my point of view, it was almost a scientific term, a natural name like "dog" or "cat" or "cow." It was simply who black people were. Yet as a white Southerner growing up in the 1950s and early 60s, I was ever aware of the foreboding presence of black people. There was something mysterious and forbidden about them. There was the "exotic" sense of the other, of course, but there was something deeper and incongruous. There was the knowledge, not brought to consciousness but rather deep in my soul, of the troubling presence of darker-skinned people, troubling not because of who they were, but troubling because of who I was.

Indeed, even though they lived only a few houses away from me in my childhood years, I had no awareness that those I called "N-word" were people like me. Though my family was relatively poor, we shared leftover food and clothing with a black family who lived down the street. In these encounters—the closest I had because I went to segregated schools—I had no idea who these people really were, but it seemed clear to me that they were not human beings like me. And it was clear that it was forbidden and dangerous to explore who they really were. As a boy, I sometimes had a sense that there was more to the story than I had been taught. I remember thinking, "What if they really are like us?" Such an exploration was dangerous because it could lead to difficult truth: they are like us; they are human beings like us. I was only a boy, and a fatherless boy at that. I was not about to take on such a dangerous exploration because I was so unsure of my own worth and my own manliness.

My father abandoned my mother and me when I was a baby. I never saw him again until I was in my twenties. Part of my struggle as a youth was this situation: I wondered why he never contacted me, never came to see me. I concluded that something must be wrong with me, that deep down, I was unworthy of being his son—and a great anxiety attached itself to my heart. One of the mitigating factors in this struggle was First Presbyterian Church in Helena—in the midst of my struggles, they sought to step into the breech. They spent time with me; nurtured me; told me that I was special. It was a great gift to me—it was what the church is supposed to be, to share God's love with those who feel unlovely. Even now I feel a warmth about the gifts of those church people—they mediated God's love to me powerfully and profoundly. As my inner voice told me that I was not worth much because my father had abandoned me, their voices told me that I had great worth because God loved me, and they loved me. The members of my church were loving, caring, and supportive of me. They were also influential people in the town who helped determine political and social policy: bankers, teachers, planters, and farmers.

And they were racists. Some were more tolerant than others, but they all believed in white supremacy, and they taught it to me. They were extremely uncomfortable when the civil rights movement came to the South. They felt that things should stay the same, that political and economic and social power should stay under white control. Few, if any, considered the idea that the black people, who made up the majority of people in our county, were human beings like them. They felt that black people should not have access to power because they felt that black people could not handle power responsibly. These good and loving people who saw such potential in me could not see the same potential in black people. From my point of view, their blinders to the humanity of black people did not negate their goodness, but it did make them racists.

I use this example as a way of helping the reader enter into my journey and into the journeys of many of us classified as "white" in the South in the 1950s and 1960s. We were thoroughly permeated by the principality of race and its ordering of the world with those classified as "white" as superior and all other race categories as "inferior." Though many dynamics have changed over these last fifty years, the power of whiteness continues—all of us in America,

especially those of us classified as "white," have had our consciousness and our humanity taken over by the power and principality of
race. The author of the Letter to the Ephesians uses this powerful
image in Ephesians 6:10–20. He describes the journey to health
and wholeness as similar to a Roman soldier getting ready for battle, and in my experience with the power of race in my own life
and in the lives of others, it is a difficult struggle. Ida Wells certainly had to put on her armor in order to wrestle with the power
of race, and she knew these verses in Ephesians.

Yet I have changed, and I am writing this in part because I
want to suggest that those of us classified as "white" can acknowledge the depth of the power of race in us, while discovering ways
to begin to move toward health and salvation. I want to share a bit
of my history of coming to awareness about what it means to be
white. I have changed, and I am struggling with my own racism;
yet I know that I will never be cured of racism. It is deeply embedded in my being, and I benefit greatly from my racial classification of "white." Those are parts of me that I am often desperate
to deny. Just as I cringed earlier when I wrote that my wonderful
grandfather was a racist, so now I cringe when I say that I am a
racist. I do not have a martyr complex, and I am not overwhelmed
with guilt. I simply want to acknowledge the continuing power
of race in me and in our culture. What is asked of those of us
who are white is not purity or even complete healing—what is
asked of us is awareness and acknowledgment and a commitment
to change. It is not only that we are afraid of sharing power with
black people—those of us classified as "white" cannot even imagine doing so. The political backlash that we all experienced after
the presidency of Barack Obama is an indication of how uncomfortable white people are with a black person having power over
us. It is the same kind of power that Ida Wells encountered in her
life. Though we have obviously made some progress, the fundamental power of "whiteness" still remains intact.

Many younger white people in America feel that racism is a problem only for older white people, that for younger white people, racism is a thing of the past. The reality is that their institutional and structural lives reflect "white" and "nonwhite" at the least, with perhaps more curiosity and more experience in engaging people marked as "browns," Asian Americans, and multiracial. From the younger point of view, the world may be more multiracial than the "black and white" world of my youth, but the central lens remains "white" and "nonwhite." Like I did, they have breathed in this perceptual apparatus, to use the intriguing phrase from the beginning of the second chapter of the Letter to the Ephesians, "power of the prince of the air." In the beginning of chapter 2 of Ephesians, Paul (or a student of Paul's) uses a "primitive" phrase to describe our captivity to the power of sin: "You were once dead through the trespasses and sins in which you once lived, following the course of this world, following the prince of the power of the air" (RSV). On one level, it sounds like an outmoded idea, perhaps useful 2,000 years ago, but outdated now. Who really believes that there is a personality called the "prince of the power of the air"?[2] If we consider its meaning in the context of the continuing power of racism, then the reality begins to sink in. We need the power of the air to breathe and live, but we also breathe in pollutants as we receive life-giving breath. One of those pollutants is the power of race, taught to us by our families, by our churches, by our communities—taught to us by those who love us. In this sense, there is no way around the power of race in our consciousness if we are raised in America, no matter our generation or our class status or our racial status. Those of us classified as "white" must always keep this dynamic before us—we learned the idea of white supremacy from those

---

2. I am indebted to Walter Wink and his work on the Powers—"Naming the Powers" (1984), "Unmasking the Powers" (1986), "Engaging the Powers" (1992)—for helping me to gain insight into the reality that this seemingly abandoned phrase is describing.

who love us. Principalities and powers like race take root most convincingly in us not at the point of a sword or the barrel of a gun but through the power of the loving people who raise us.

For the American context, it begins in the desire to remove the native peoples and to hold slaves and to remain Christians, all at the same time. It is a powerful theme in American history. How could we commit genocide and hold slaves and call ourselves Christian? We did it by moving Jesus out of the world. We emphasized that all God (and Jesus) cared about was the eternal status of individual souls. This movement had staying power for obvious reasons—we asserted that the God revealed in the life, death, and resurrection of Jesus of Nazareth was not particularly interested in our being witnesses for transformation and justice in this life. God was only interested in our personal and individual passage from this life into eternal life. So, yes, we who were classified as white could take land and hold slaves and be Christians. Many of our white forebears argued that not only could we hold slaves and be followers of Jesus—many argued that God had ordained white supremacy and genocide and slavery. This system offered something for everyone—for those of us classified as white, we were able to leave God in heaven, and all was right in the world, including and especially slavery. For African Americans held as slaves, who were treated so inhumanely and so unjustly, the idea of life after death being the main point of Christianity had deep resonance. Justice would be meted out then if not in this life.

Perhaps this feels to be ancient history and not applicable anymore except as a distant memory. The social media postings of police violence toward black and Latinx men and women—and the election of Donald Trump as president—remind us that this is still a powerful and viable system. While that system has ever been so powerful and continues to be, the election of an African American man as president shook many white people to our core. We seem to have been determined to restore "white-ness" to the "White" House, and we did.

The system of race remains as it has been from the beginning—a political construct used as a means of distributing power. While legal segregation may have ended for the most part, the "dog whistles" of race remain strong.[3] Race is not based in biology or genetics or theology or even culture—it is based in social con-structs designed to keep those classified as "white" in privilege and power, while making it exceedingly difficult for all other racial classifications to break into privilege and power. Many of us who are white are determined to restore clearly and forcefully the idea that has been at our center since the European begin-nings of the nation: whiteness is the center of life as an American.

Yet it is possible to change, because God's Spirit will not be defeated by our captivity to the powers and principalities. Just as my family participated in racism and taught it to me, my fam-ily also sought some freedom from it for me. I experienced this struggle clearly in my mother. She was a Southern white woman, born and raised in Marshall County, Mississippi. She raised me as a single mom, working six days a week as a beauty operator. She taught me racism, but in the midst of the lessons, she also sought, in her own way, to emphasize the humanity of all people. She would not allow me to call black adults by their first names, and I would get irritated at her for this, because so many of my white friends did. She simply said that all adults would be "Mister or Miss." I also remember one particular episode that related to Jewish people. I don't remember how old I was, but I remember coming home from school with a searing hatred of Jews. When my mother came home from work, I told her, "I hate Jews." She asked me why I would say that, and I replied that I hated them

---

3. Ian Haney Lopez, *Dog Whistle Politics: How Coded Racial Appeals Have Reinvented Racism* (New York: Oxford University Press, 2014).

just because they were Jews. She replied: "But you don't hate Raymond, do you?" I said: "No, he's one of my friends!" "What about Ruth?" she asked. "Oh, well, she's a girl, but she's nice." Then my mother summed it up: "Nibs, they are both Jewish. Do you hate them too?" I was shocked! "No, Mother, I don't hate them." She then delivered the fast ball: "Well, Nibs, I think that you had better be careful about whom you think that you hate." The world became more complicated at that point, and while I pondered that, I also began to think that I needed to be more careful about what I told my mother![4]

A second source of awareness was my church. I have already indicated their gifts to me. Despite their teaching me racism, they also taught me that serving God is first and foremost in our lives. The love that my church shared with me helped me to understand that God is alive, that the gospel is powerful, and that the gospel's view of life takes precedence over the world's view of life. When the time came to make a decision on race, I could consider the possibility that God wanted something different than a white worldview, even if it meant conflict with those very church members who had nurtured this thought process in me.

A third source of awareness were teachers in my segregated public school, with one teacher, Vera Miller, standing out. She encouraged us to see a different worldview, to understand that there was a bigger world out there than the one we experienced in the white South. She taught English, and she was Jewish, and perhaps out of that sense of being an "outsider," she wanted us to see a different and deeper world. I'd also like to think that she, like Jesus the Jew, was driven by the Jewish prophetic tradition, which emphasized justice rolling down like waters and righteousness, like an everflowing stream. I don't remember

---

4. Some of this biographical material appeared previously in Nibs Stroupe and Inez Fleming, *While We Run This Race* (Maryknoll, NY: Orbis Books, 1995), 92–102.

how we started the conversation, but one day after class, she suggested that I read *Cry, the Beloved Country* by Alan Paton.[5] I had never heard of it, but she explained that a white South African wrote it about the apartheid situation in that country. Since I respected her so much, I got the book and read it, and it opened a crack in my worldview.

In that book, I met my first black person. I say "person," because although I saw black people all the time in my town, I never considered that they might be human beings like me until I met the Reverend Steven Kumalo in Alan Paton's book. Reverend Kumalo was a pastor in the rural area who went searching for his son, who had left the rural area for the city and work. It was a painful search for him, and though I have never identified why the connection to me was so deeply felt, I am guessing that it was the estrangement between father and son that grabbed me. I was the reverse of Reverend Kumalo. I was always looking for my father, feeling the pain of his loss, hoping, hoping, hoping that he was coming for me, but he never did. He's not coming for me. Yet here Reverend Kumalo was coming for his son and, for the first time, I remember thinking: "Black people may be human beings like me." It is a sad admission but a true one—I met my first black person as a fictional character in a book. I went back and read that book this past summer, and for the first time, it hit me: Reverend Kumalo was a character created by a white man, and as I shook my head at that irony, it also gave me hope that perhaps I can reach white people in this book, not by creating characters but sharing some of my story and the power of race in my life.

Paton's book made a little crack in my view of the world and opened my eyes just a bit. The next marker that I recall was Martin Luther King's "I Have Dream" speech in August 1963 at the March on Washington. I had learned and accepted the view that

5. Alan Paton, *Cry the Beloved Country* (New York: Charles Scribner's Sons, 1950).

Dr. King was a communist, or at least was being duped by the communists. The secondary view was that he was just making money off unsuspecting and "simple" black people. His speech took place a week before I would begin my senior year in high school, and I decided to listen to the speech on television in the safety of my home, with none of my friends around. I did not want to be considered to be a "N-lover." I listened to Dr. King's speech, and I was astonished. His eloquence and passion were powerful, and I simply could not believe that all the 250,000 people in attendance were being duped by him. There seemed to be another part of the story that I had somehow missed, and I began to think about how to find out. I was still fatherless and anxious, however, so I had to have covert activities, and I began to dip my toes in some different waters.

A fourth source of awareness for me was my friendship with high school classmate David Billings. Though we were quite different, we resonated on many levels, and he and I served as colleagues and guides and explorers together in this new world. We remain friends today, and I do not believe that I would have had the courage to stretch as much as I began to do if he and I had not been friends and shared this journey. Please get his fine book *Deep Denial: The Persistence of White Supremacy in United States History and Life.*[6] I remember the turning point well. In Helena at the end of Christmas break of our sophomore year in college, we were discussing our future. We had both done manual labor in Helena the summer before, and as we approached the summer after our sophomore year, we wanted to stretch ourselves and try something new, especially something less physically strenuous. As we considered various options, I said that I had heard of a church in Brooklyn that hired college students for its summer work in

---

6. David Billings, *Deep Denial: The Persistence of White Supremacy in United States History and Life* (Roselle, NJ: Crandall, Dostie and Douglass Books, 2016).

Bedford-Stuyvesant. David's aunt Peggy Billings lived in New York, and that made it sound possible. We agreed that I would investigate the possibilities and get back in touch with him. In the meantime, two small-town Southern boys dreamed of the glamour and possibilities of New York City.

We were both accepted as members of the church's summer program, and the time at Lafayette Avenue Presbyterian Church in 1966 was an experience that changed our lives. For the first time ever, we worked with African Americans as peers, and our supervisors were African American. As Southern white boys captured by racism, we experienced the gift of a moment when those whom we had seen as "other" became people and indeed our leaders. Our understanding of ourselves and of the world was changed forever. We were in the presence of African Americans as people, as human beings like us. There were many miles to go in our consciousness, of course, but David and I would never be the same again. When I came back to the South from Brooklyn that summer, I saw life differently. The dissonance was so great between Helena and Brooklyn, and at first I tried to believe that the African American people whom I had met in Brooklyn were qualitatively different from the black people in Helena. I had been changed, but I still wanted to hold on to the white opinions that I had held so long. My eyes had been opened, however, and those former opinions could no longer hold me. A shift had taken place—the world did not look the same. I could not go back to my former consciousness. The journey had definitely begun.

When I returned to my hometown at the end of that summer, I shared with my church the excitement of what had been revealed to me in Brooklyn. I felt that the church leaders had simply been ignorant, and that my revelatory experience would help convince them of a new truth. Instead of being met with the enthusiasm that I had expected, I was received with stern resistance. The reaction was that I had gone up North and had been perverted by the

Yankees—an old story for white Southerners. My soul was in turmoil because the church, one of my important parenting figures, rejected both the power and the accuracy of my revelatory experience. This rejection opened a deep chasm in my heart. I was attentive to this process, but I felt that I had crossed over, and the main work had been done. It was the typical response of those of us who are white, who have had some sort of conversion experience on race. I simply did not realize how deeply race was part of my identity. I would have miles and miles to go before I sleep, and I still do.

That brings me to the fifth source of my awareness—the numerous people of color (especially African Americans) who have been willing to engage me in this journey, those willing to listen to me, to challenge me, to befriend me, to allow themselves to be vulnerable with me. I have been privileged to receive gifts from them in Brooklyn, in college, in seminary, in church work, but most especially in my long pastorate at Oakhurst Presbyterian Church in Decatur, with my spouse and copastor the Reverend Caroline Leach. Oakhurst is a place where so many kinds of different people have come together to struggle and to seek to find a new way to be human beings together, as children of God. I have made many mistakes, too numerous to enumerate, but so many folk have been willing to take me on and to help to develop me and educate me and to help me recover my humanity. I will weave some of those stories into this book, but for now, I just want to say "Thank you."[7]

Into this system in my life came Ida B. Wells. In the fall of 1985, I decided to preach on Black History Month in February 1986. My approach would be to find witnesses who had worked for racial justice and equity throughout American history and to feature them in my weekly sermons in February. My guidelines would be to focus primarily on African Americans, to choose

---

7. Nibs Stroupe and Caroline Leach, *O Lord, Hold Our Hands: How a Church Thrives in a Multicultural World* (Louisville, KY: Westminster/JohnKnox Press, 2003), 46–55.

people who had already died, and to blend in well-known witnesses (such as Frederick Douglass and Harriet Tubman) with
lesser known witnesses. Fortunately for me as a Presbyterian, the
subjects and scripture lessons for weekly sermons are under the
sole authority of the pastor, so I had some cover there, and it
worked! I continued doing this from 1986 through my retirement in 2017.

In order to prepare for this sermon series in 1986, I began to
do research on witnesses for racial justice and equity. One of the
first books that I read was *Black Foremothers* by Dorothy Sterling.[8]
Three women were featured in that book: Mary Church Terrell,
Ellen Craft, and Ida Wells. I preached on all three of them over the
years, but the story of Ida Wells went deeply into my soul. She was
a powerful witness, and I had never heard of her! Part of that lack
was my own ignorance and white arrogance, that I thought that
I knew much more than I did. Part of it was the sexism that rolls
through American history—she was a woman who was a powerful
witness, and yet in 1985, she had largely been forgotten in American history and in the history of racial justice. She had been prom-
inently known in her day—indeed, the *New York Times* announced
her wedding to Frederick Barnett in 1895 on the front page of its
Style section. But then she was lost—the *Times* had nothing about
her passing in 1931.[9] Thanks to her daughter Alfreda Duster's editing of her autobiography and to several books like Paula Giddings
Sword Among the Lions, she has been recovered and is now among
the pantheon of important witnesses.

It was not just my ignorance of Ida Wells that struck me
in this encounter in 1985. She was born in 1862 in the same
county as all my forebears—Marshall County, Mississippi. She

---

8. Sterling, *Black Foremothers*, 61–118.

9. Nikole Hannah-Jones, "When Ida B. Wells Married, It Was a Page One Story," *New York Times*, January 23, 2017.

and my great-great-great-grandmother were likely contemporaries, though I would be stunned if they knew one another. As I indicated earlier, my ancestors owned people as slaves, and great-great-great-grandmother was one of those owners. Still, it struck me that they lived at the same time and in the same place but in entirely different worlds, just as Catherine and I lived in the same but different spaces. In the summer of 2015, I met with Michelle Duster in Chicago to talk about Ida Wells. We met in a restaurant located in the district represented by Barack Obama when he had been a state senator in Illinois. She is the great-granddaughter of Ida Wells, and it was a humbling experience to talk with her and feel Ida Wells's spirit in her. It was also humbling to feel the slave-holding spirit residing in me, all the while feeling the warmth of the stories that I had heard about my relatives in my mother's side of the family.

Wells also spent time in Memphis, teaching and writing, and Memphis was the city to which my family related during my childhood, even though we lived in eastern Arkansas. For many seasons Memphis has been the capital of east Arkansas, north Mississippi, and west Tennessee. I also attended college in Memphis and there began experiencing and practicing my shift in my relationship to race. Memphis also was the place that radicalized Ida Wells on lynching. After her friend Tom Moss was lynched in Memphis in 1892, she made a dramatic shift in becoming a public person.

This coincidence of history is important to me, but what makes Ida Wells stand out for me is her stunning witness for justice over the course of fifty years. She was a relentless fighter for racial, gender, and economic justice and walked in "intersectionality" long before it became a modern term. After I discovered her in 1985, I found a copy of her *Crusade for Justice* and devoured it and became an Ida Wells devotee. As I noted earlier, my first discovery of the humanity of people classified as "black" came from a character in a book, and likewise, my discovery of the power of Reconstruction and the stripping down and discrediting of that period in order to reestablish slavery came from my encounter with the life and story of Ida Wells. I had been raised by white Southern culture to believe that the period of Reconstruction failed because black people were unable to handle power. The life of Ida Wells taught me an entirely different story: Reconstruction failed because white people did not want to share power with black people. It failed because white Southerners systematically terrorized black people and white allies in order to reestablish slavery in the South after the Civil War. The life and witness of Ida Wells opened this door for me to see a deeper and more realistic picture of an era about which I had been completely wrong. Her powerful witness pulled me back into American history in a way that I had never imagined before. I want to weave this theme of continuing white supremacy with Ida Wells's story together now to explain why she is such a powerful witness to me, and why she should be such a powerful witness to others.

Her geographical connection to my family history is the beginning point for me. All of my folks were from Byhalia and Cayce in Mississippi, while she was from Holly Springs. Both towns are in Marshall County, which I know well, although my initial feeling of fame was that William Faulkner had died there. When I discovered Wells's birthplace and date, I felt that familial Southern connection that is woven, for better or for worse, through Southern history. Her diminutive stature and her determination reminded me of my mother, especially with both of them having difficult family issues, which they handled with iron wills and fortitude. Even though Ida Wells was exiled from the South for the majority of her life, I still feel that connection crossing time and race and gender and geography.

The white Southern narrative about Reconstruction designated that period of history to be a failure because African Americans were genetically and culturally unable to handle power well.

That narrative has imprinted itself not just on white Southern consciousness but on the national consciousness as well. The life and witness of Ida Wells serves as counter to that narrative, and we would all do well to learn from her. As I encountered her, I read W. E. B. Du Bois's *Black Reconstruction in America* and Eric Foner's *Reconstruction: America's Unfinished Revolution*.[10] In these books and others, I had ears to hear, to use Jesus's phrase in his description of the ability to comprehend the meaning of his parables. I had begun to debunk the propaganda of Reconstruction on which I had been raised, but my encounter with the life of Ida Wells now made that journey personal. Her story enabled me to see the great lie of the white narrative of Reconstruction and post-Reconstruction. Her integrity and her determination and her humanity helped me to reorient my view of Reconstruction. Her journey also enabled me to see that the "neo-slavery" in which I was raised was of the same kind that crushed the democratic experiment of Reconstruction. The segregation and neo-slavery of the 1940s and 1950s was a continuation of the white supremacy power that has been so strong throughout the European history of this country. My encounter with Ida B. Wells helped me to reorient my view of race and myself and my complicity in the systematic American story of the development of white supremacy, a development that is regaining strength as I write these pages.

A third characteristic of Ida Wells is that she refused to internalize the definitions of racism that white supremacy sought to place on her. White supremacy works best when those who are being oppressed accept that they should be oppressed, that there is something in their individual or cultural nature that compels them to be oppressed. This is why the election of Barack Obama as president of

---

10. W. E. B. Du Bois, *Black Reconstruction in America* (New York: Atheneum, 1935, 1962), and Eric Foner, *Reconstruction: America's Unfinished Revolution* (New York: Harper-Collins, 1988).

the United States threatened so many people classified as "white." If a person of color can be elected as president, it belies the idea of the inferiority of people of color. It was not just African Americans who were stunned by the election of Barack Obama. White folks were stunned too, but in a different way. The election of Barack Obama undercut one of the foundations of white supremacy: the idea of black inferiority. This shaking of the foundations led to the election of what Ta-Nehisi Coates calls the "first white president" of the United States.[11] By this, Coates means that in the 2016 election, white Americans consciously chose someone whose only qualification to be president was that he was classified as "white."

The election of Donald Trump as president not only told everyone that the office was reserved for white men—it also sought to tell people of color to get back into their usual place in the hierarchy of white supremacy, below those classified as "white." This is how it works. Dr. Gayraud Wilmore and I cochaired the Committee to Combat Racism of Greater Atlanta Presbytery from 1995 to 2001. We sought to find ways to combat the power of racism in the church and in the larger world. One of the processes that we used was to hold hearings on how racism had impacted all of our lives. At one of those hearings, the Rev. Lonnie Oliver talked about being one of three African Americans who integrated the white high schools in Hampton, Virginia, in 1963.[12] He was a good student and a star athlete, and his parents and his culture had always taught him that he was a child of God, that the lie of white racism that he was inferior was just that: a lie. As far as he knew, he had not internalized inferiority, as he was supposed to do. The system of race works best when those classified as "white" internalize that we are superior, the "IRS" (Internalized Racial Superiority, as my friend and

---

11. Ta-Nehisi Coates, *We Were Eight Years in Power* (New York: One World, 2017), 341.

12. Rev. Lonnie Oliver, Task Force on Racism Hearings, Presbytery of Greater Atlanta, June 10, 2000.

colleague David Billings calls it).[13] Accompanying this is the desire for people of color to internalize that they are inferior (IRI), thus allowing white folks to claim that the system of race and racism are natural, are God-given. Reverend Oliver gave thanks that he seemed to have avoided this internalized racial inferiority. Yet in his testimony that day, he noted a powerful story in his journey of integration. He and his fellow white football players had just received the results of their first quiz in biology. He asked his white teammates what their scores were, and he was shocked to hear that they had scored lower than he had. He testified that he felt an electric shock go through him as he heard their scores. He was shocked to hear that he had scored higher, and he did not know the source of this amazement, because he had been taught all his life that he was the equal of white people. Still, the idea of white supremacy had permeated his consciousness so much so that when evidence came to the contrary, he felt an electric jolt.

Ida Wells never accepted this idea of white supremacy. This affirmation of her equal humanity made her a vocal and fierce opponent of the system of race and the white supremacy that flowed from it. The reason that her writings on lynching were so offensive to white folks was that she asserted that the cause of the lynchings had nothing to do with black male lasciviousness, but it had everything to do with white racism and with the terrorism to crush black life. She was in the face of white supremacy, and this is what made her so dangerous that a high price was put on her head by the white people of Memphis. We are in a time now when the white ridicule of people of color, especially those classified as "black," is increasing, with the hope that people of color will internalize this system. We need the fierce witness and voice of Ida Wells as much as ever.

---

13. Billings, *Deep Denial*, 6.

One of the powerful parts of the witness of Ida Wells is that she refused to yield to the power of racism. She refused to resign herself to its power, and her entire adult life seems to have been rooted in the desire to push back against the power of racism and to seek to diminish its power. She didn't win many victories in the fight with racism, but she was never defeated. From her first direct engagement with institutional racism in the train car in 1884, to the lynching of her friends in Memphis in 1892, to the protest at the Columbian Exposition in 1893 in Chicago because it refused to acknowledge the accomplishments or heritage of people of African descent, she stayed in the fray and never gave up. She made two trips to Great Britain to combat racism and to seek support for her antilynching campaign, and even after marrying Ferdinand Barnett in 1895 and having children, she remained in the struggle to overcome the power of racism for herself, for her fellow African Americans, and for all of us. She was a founding member of the NAACP, even though the sexism of the black leaders kept her out of a leadership position. She met with President Woodrow Wilson to seek to keep him, as the first white Southerner elected president since the Civil War, from resegregating the federal government. She lost that battle, but she was never defeated.

Ida Wells was "intersectional" before it became cool and topical. She raised her siblings after the death of her parents, and then she raised her own four children after marrying at the age of thirty-three (a late marriage in those days). She worked as hard as she could in her "divided duty," as we saw Susan B. Anthony name it. She also refused to take a step back in fighting for women's rights. She understood the great stress that black men were under from the decimation and violence of racism, but she would not yield to the men in order to lift them up in a white, racist society. She labored hard and long for the rights of black men, but she would not allow that fight to deter or to defer rights for black women. Part of the reason that she was in danger of being forgotten was that she alienated so many black men with her defiant affirmation of the equality of black women.

As we approach the hundredth anniversary of the passage of the Nineteenth Amendment, which gave women the right to vote in 1920, we would do well to remember how racist some of those white women often were in their fight for the vote for women. In many of their minds, this right to vote for women meant "white" women only. Even those who were sympathetic for votes for black women were often afraid to allow black women's leadership in the suffragist movement, because they did not want to alienate white southern women who were supporters of the passage of the Nineteenth Amendment. Ida Wells had joined the white-led Women's Suffrage Association early in her Chicago life. In 1913, she founded the Alpha Suffrage Club, the first Illinois suffrage organization for black women. Later that year, when she sought to join the national women's parade for voting rights for women on the day before Woodrow Wilson was inaugurated as president, she was forbidden by Alice Paul and others to march with the white leadership, because they felt that her black presence might offend southern white women supporters. The Illinois delegation supported her, though, and when their section passed by in the march, she stepped in to join them. A supporter noted the incident with a small poem that began:

> Side by side with the whites she walked,
> Step by step the Southerners balked,
> But Illinois, fond of order and grace,
> Stuck to the black Queen of our race.[14]

Ida Wells felt a great commitment to both the necessity and the building of community through churches, clubs, and

---

14. Sterling, *Black Foremothers*, 110.

leagues. Although she was a strong individual, she also perceived the importance of building groups and associations that could wield political and social power, especially in a racist world where individuals could easily be dominated and picked off. She was a committed and active member of churches, first in the African Methodist Episcopal Church, then in the Presbyterian Church. In her churches she worked to form associations for women to develop a civic duty, a sense of the importance of social and political engagement by women in a world which told them that such activities were useless. In 1895, she helped to organize the Ida B. Wells Club as part of the black women's civic club movement that had started with Josephine Ruffington in Boston. She was always aware of the necessity of building community to help protect individuals who were oppressed and to help build political power to seek to mitigate that oppression, whether it was racial or gender or economic oppression.

After the white Springfield riots in 1908, in which three African Americans were lynched in the town where Abraham Lincoln rose to the presidency, she initiated the Negro Fellowship League out of the men's Sunday school class that she taught in Grace Presbyterian Church. Its purpose was to reinvigorate the movement to abolish lynching in Illinois and to help those caught in the terrible jaws of racism. As African Americans continued to migrate from the South to escape the overt oppression there, the League expanded to develop a house where migrants could find temporary housing and could learn the ways of their new home. Ida Wells gained a job as a probation officer during this time, and she used her salary to fund the house. In developing these clubs and more on a national level, Wells combined two important elements in fighting racism and other forms of oppression. There is the element of working for justice, seeking to change political structures and institutions, so that they will be oriented toward justice and equity rather than toward injustice and exploitation.

Ida Wells was clearly a leader in this element, both locally and nationally. The second element is charity, which is the "feet on the ground" approach. Many activists often consider this charity work to be relatively unimportant, but Wells saw it as essential to assist those who were caught in the snares of racism and sexism. For most of its existence, she visited the Fellowship League house on State Street on a daily basis. She emphasized that this charity work was inextricably linked with the work for justice, that each informed and invigorated the other.

Ida Wells was fearless, ferocious, formidable, and a feminist. I like this alliteration, but today Wells would likely respond that she was "womanist," not "feminist," in order to note the differences and tensions between white women and women of color, especially women classified as "black."[15] Of course she knew fear, but she did not allow herself to be dominated by anxiety. She took herself into places that were scary and dangerous, but "nevertheless, she persisted." Such a witness is important for herself and for others. It was a vision and a power that made her a powerful witness in whatever area she worked. As a poster put it recently in the Belmont-Paul Women's house in Washington, DC, "you can't spell 'formidable' without Ida B."[16]

We have the witness of Ida B. Wells, reminding us that in this time, and indeed in any time, we are always called to be to be fearless, ferocious, formidable, and feminist. "Fearless" because the powers of racism and sexism and materialism and others want us to be dominated by fear, to have anxiety at our core, so that we will be afraid to speak and act on behalf of justice and equity. "Ferocious" because the powers will roar at us and seek to make us timid in the face of its power. The witness of Ida Wells echoes

15. Jacquelyn Grant, *White Women's Christ and Black Women's Jesus* (Atlanta: Scholars Press, 1989).

16. Visit to Belmont-Paul National Women's Monument, Washington, DC, August 23, 2018.

to us to remain steadfast in our consciousness and in our work, and whether we will feel as if we are ferocious or not, the world will see us as such.

"Formidable" because our keeping our integrity and persistence in the face of race and other powers will make us seem much more powerful than we actually may be. Our culture of white supremacy is not accustomed to people of any racial category standing up and proclaiming a different way. If we do this, we will be magnified, and as our friend Ed Loring puts it, "If you want to get to heaven, you have to raise a little hell."

"Feminist" because Ida Wells's witness reminds us of the importance of "intersectionality," the reality that many categories overlap and inform one another in the areas of oppression and liberation. Wells knew well that it was just as important to free women of all racial categories from male dominance as it was to free those classified as "black" from racial oppression—all included, no one left behind. This affirmation of women's rights cost Wells dearly in the work for justice, but she would not yield on this.

In 1917, there was a race riot in Houston. It resulted from the neo-slavery treatment of black soldiers stationed in nearby Camp Logan. The soldiers marched defiantly into Houston, daring white folks to mess with them, and eventually the shooting began. Several white persons, including police officers, were killed. Twelve African American soldiers were tried and hung for their part in the riot. Ida Wells wanted to hold a memorial service for these soldiers in Chicago, and she felt certain that she could find a black church that would host it. Yet all the male pastors declined. Having no place to hold the service, she decided to have buttons made, protesting the injustice. It did not take long for the Secret Service to show up and inquire about the buttons and to ask her to cease and desist distributing them, lest she be arrested for treason. Here is her account about it in her *Crusade for Justice*:

"Well," said the shorter of the two men, "the rest of your people do not agree with you." I said, "Maybe not. They don't know any better, or they are afraid of losing their whole skins. As for myself, I don't care. I'd rather go down in history as one lone Negro who dared to tell the government that it had done a dastardly thing than to save my skin by taking back what I have said. I would consider it an honor to spend whatever years are necessary in prison as the one member of the race who protested, rather than to be with the 11,999,999 Negroes who didn't have to go to prison because they kept their mouths shut. Lay on, Macduff, and damn'd be him that first cries, 'Hold, enough!'"[17]

They did not arrest her, and she kept distributing the buttons. No wonder she seems so formidable and unbelievable— no wonder we sought to erase her from our history. No wonder that we need to draw from her life and witness so much right now. She understood the connection between Jesus and us. The ministry of Jesus happened in the system of oppression known as the Roman Empire, a system that looks remarkably like white male supremacy in our own day. Jesus came to liberate us all— oppressed and oppressors—from this system, and I give thanks that Ida B. Wells understood this and sought to live it out.

Questions for Further Reflection

1. How has the power of race impacted your life?
2. Where have you worked to change that impact?
3. If you have not worked to change it, what has prevented you from doing it?

---

17. Duster, *Crusade*, 370.

CHAPTER 5

"At the Crossroads: Just Trying to Be Human"

African Americans stand at the crossroads where our understanding of race and gender intersect. But that intersection is complicated by the age-old negative supremacist narratives about their humanity. Wells's work still shines brilliantly into this darkness and contributes to our effort to explore these challenging dynamics.

In the preface to the book *On Lynchings*, Wells makes an important statement in response to the narrative that spoke of blacks as beast, "The Afro-American is not a bestial race. If this work can contribute in any way toward proving this, and at the same time arouse the conscience of the American people to a demand for justice to every citizen, and punishment by law for the lawless, I shall feel I have done my race a service. Other considerations are of minor importance."[1]

Wells understood that African Americans have been challenged with the dilemma of being seen as human since arriving on the soil in this country. The slave holders had to make the Africans that they held in slavery "the other" in order to justify slavery. Thus the internal and social mandate requiring justification for their indefensible system of holding another human being in bondage led to

---

Although "At the Crossroads" is written from a third-person perspective, the author is Catherine Meeks.

1. Ida B. Wells-Barnett, *On Lynchings* (New York: Humanity Books, 2002), 17.

the "beast scenario." This narrative was forged from the beginning of slavery; all of the structures for control which were imagined and instituted were created to serve the beast narrative. As time continued and the narrative met resistance to it from the enslaved, another characterization was born. The idea of the "extraordinary Negro" emerged. This is the person who is often considered to be a "credit to the race" and who is upheld as the exception. Of course, there are only a few people of African descent who can occupy this space. The concept serves the white supremacist's view because it maintains control and also allows that mind to rationalize any tiny acts of civility toward the black person. Since those acts are reserved for the "extraordinary Negro," other acts of violence and repression can continue to be justified.

As long as the narrative of "other" can be supported, the possibility of maintaining the white supremacy paradigm is protected. This way of constructing reality makes possible the attitudes and behaviors that are currently being expressed.

Wells's life and work bore witness to another way to see reality. One did not have to choose between being a "beast" or "extraordinary" and she spent her life standing against that narrative. Unfortunately, she had to stand against it both as a person of African descent and as a female. Just as black men and women were not seen as full human beings, neither were black women seen as women. Wells was a woman with all of the foibles of every other human. She embarked upon her earthly journey with tenacious courage and sought to create the same opportunity for all of her sisters and brothers. She understood that the journey to liberation was not about splitting oneself into categories of black or white, male or female, but of incorporating the whole person in the journey. Thus, the journey of liberation had to be traveled as a whole person embodying all of the characteristics that made one an individual, including race and gender.

White women thought that the suffrage movement could be separated from concerns for the welfare of black women. The white women's feminist movement continues to leave black women behind because there is more interest in addressing oppression around gender than race.

The amazing challenge that black women faced during Wells's era (and continue to face) was that they could not stand up for justice for themselves as women without struggling for the liberation of their husbands, uncles, fathers, brothers, and sons. This effort at dividing the loyalty between race and gender was insufficient to speak to the challenge facing the African American woman then as now.

Of course, black women have to labor against the patriarchal oppression that exists within the race as black men learned the gender inequality narrative very well, but the resistance against gender oppression does not erase the need to stay the course in the quest for racial freedom. The fact that Wells understood this so well and engaged the work of liberation on both fronts is a great gift to the struggle that we continue to face in the twenty-first century. The black woman has the continuing dilemma of being challenged to choose between the two. Wells knew, as do all of us who engage the fight for liberation today, that there is no choice to be made. One cannot split one's sense of moral outrage into categories. To claim to want to forge the path to racial freedom without caring about gender freedom and freedom from all oppression is to create a false dichotomy.

During the Black Liberation Struggle of the 1960s and early 1970s, the charge was made in some circles that the quest for gender liberation by black women was the assumption of a misguided agenda set forth by white women. Many black women knew that analysis was not correct and that to the extent that black men proposed it, they had to be resisted in that regard. Thus, the agenda of the women in that era, just as it was for

Wells, was to stand against black men in their gender oppression and for them in the quest for racial liberation.

This dilemma is a source of painful conflict. It creates a lonely space for black women who have opened their minds and hearts to understand that one does not get to pick and choose in the liberation struggle. Both racial and gender oppression have to be engaged. The additional challenge is that of being rendered invisible in both the racial liberation and gender liberation movements. Despite Toni Morrison's observation about black women's ability to invent themselves,[2] this process does not make the black woman extraordinary; it simply allows her to be human and to fight against the invisibility blues that hound her throughout her lifetime.

As a young woman in college, Catherine worshipped with a predominately white house church congregation that had a small number of black men in it. The group loved her as best they could given their unconsciousness about their white supremacist mentality. They could not see her as black or female. They had no understanding of her life. Their focus, not unlike so many religious groups, was on the spiritual, as if one can separate the physical manifestation of oneself from a viable spiritual journey on this earth. This "invisibility"—of her blackness, her femaleness, her humanity—is the shadow side of the claim to see neither race nor gender in the other.

Wells had to confront a similar inability to be seen as she worked with Susan B. Anthony. Wells noticed that Anthony kept saying her married name with a "bite" and she asked, "Miss Anthony, don't you believe in women getting married?" Anthony responded, "Oh yes, but not women like you who have a special call for special work. . . . Since you have gotten married, agitation seems practically to have ceased. You have divided duty.

2. Toni Morrison, "What the Black Woman Thinks of Women's Lib," *New York Times*, August 22, 1971, *https://www.nytimes.com/1971/08/22/archives/what-the-black-woman-thinks-about-womens-lib-the-black-woman-and.html.*

You are here trying to help in the formation of this league and your eleven-month-old baby needs your attention. You are distracted. . . . You have divided duty." Wells responds, "Although it was a well-merited rebuke from her point of view, I could not tell Miss Anthony that it was because I was unable like herself, to get support which was necessary to carry on my work that I had become discouraged in the effort to carry on alone."[3]

Anthony did not know anything about Wells, though she had fired her stenographer for refusing to take notes for her. She related mostly to her projection of Wells. She created her own narrative of the "extraordinary person" who was only someone to help to achieve her gender-centered agenda. While Anthony saw Wells as a woman with a special call, she struggled with what she considered Wells's "divided duty" as a human being who got married and had a baby. Anthony does not see her any better than that little group of Southern California house church participants were able to see Catherine as the person she was instead of the one that they invented. So they were so shocked at her engagement in campus activism around the death of the young man described in an earlier chapter. They were not only shocked, they seemed betrayed. In some ways, one can hear a sense of betrayal in Anthony's words to Wells also.

These expressions are simply another rendition of a supremacist attitude that allows white people to think that it is clearer to them what the black persons needs than it is to those persons themselves. What a spirit of arrogance. As we listen to Wells speak about the lack of ability to get adequate support for her work and the discouragement that accompanied that lack as well as the loneliness surrounding that space that she was forced to occupy, one is deeply moved. It is not easy to be as kind in our response to that denigrating behavior as Wells was in regard to

---

3. Duster, *Crusade*, 255.

Anthony. Though Anthony was able to garner the support that she needed and to find the way to manage as a single woman who pursued the work of liberating women, she is not on record as trying to understand what Wells had to bear. Wells knew that she could not explain herself because it would not be heard. She did not have a relationship of equality with Anthony. Though it is tempting to argue that the times did not allow for the type of equity that would have made it possible for Wells to speak her truth—and that is partially true—it continues to be true that black women do not have many arenas in this present moment where their truth is welcome.

If the invisibility blues had been erased in the nineteenth century or even the twentieth century, it would be easier for black women to live the liberated lives that were intended for them today. Of course, there will be voices protesting that white women are not liberated either. While it is true that there is much work to be done so that all women can be treated as they deserve to be treated, white women do not have the same struggles ahead of them that face black women. In addition to the journey being different, black women are confronted by the racism of white women and the ways in which that racism often relegates them to a seat in the back of the room.

Just as a relationship of equality between Anthony and Wells was thwarted in their era, it continues to be the case. Along with invisibility blues is the question of black woman power in general. There are too many white women who believe themselves to be progressive and who think that they are far more liberated than white men; they are laboring under an illusion. The reality of their lack of liberation becomes apparent in the face of the power of black women. In those interactions between white women and black women who are clearly waging a struggle against both racist and sexist oppression, white women must often be included in the black woman's resistance against racism.

Catherine's own experiences bear witness to this truth as well as the innumerable stories told by powerful black women across many years of the challenges of having positions of power and authority accepted by white women. When it does happen, the path to acceptance of equality is often forged through much hard work. This hard work requires white women withdrawing their supremacist projections and black women being willing to stay in the conversation until their power is respected and accepted. It is a complex exercise and too often there is a lack of willingness to engage in the conversation long enough for a resolution favorable to everyone.

The dynamic between white women and black women is complicated by the lack of ability to stand in solidarity against racism. The powerful example from Wells's life about this issue is vividly depicted in the instance of white women in the women's suffrage movement march in Washington in 1913 expecting her not to march with the Illinois delegation of white woman. The belief was that black women needed to march at the end of the group by themselves and while the Delta Theta Sigma Sorority agreed to do so, Wells refused. The intersection of race and gender continues to present itself, as many white women still respect this type of compartmentalization. Unless there is genuine self-reflective interrogation, it is easy to be bound by the old narratives of difference and otherness, which lead to a response of resistance to black female power and presence. Actually this dynamic simply points to the insidious nature of racism. While it appears that white and black women would be able to stand together in absolute and total solidarity against the abuses of women by the structures of patriarchy, it is not true: skin color and the narrative of superiority of white skin seems to dominate too often.

Just as black women did not find an ally in white women during slavery when they were being considered as less than human, that denigration is still functioning in our world. White women must be willing to name it and actively offer great encouragement to black women. Clearly, it is not an easy task to do the required inner work to move past the temptation to see those who are different as "others" to be feared or revered in ways that mask their simple humanity.

This chapter began discussing the necessity to allow people of African descent to be acknowledged as fully human and for that to be enough for their treatment as equals. Perhaps that is the absolute core of the liberation struggle. All of us must assert the worthiness of every human being to be a free person with every right to pursue their life in their choice of ways. It appears that human beings have an innate appetite for highlighting distinctions rather than embracing commonalities.

The difference between the Africans and the Europeans made such projection so easy. The ways of the Africans were fascinating to the Europeans, who showed up in their homeland with an air of superiority. The Europeans began to name what they saw and experienced without the ability to accept those who did not choose to live as they did. The projections around the encountered differences made it easy to devalue the people on the bases of projection instead of any real understanding of African cultures. Some of this inability resulted from the Europeans calling themselves explorers, thinking of themselves as discovering the Africans as if they had not existed before the Europeans' arrival. The people in Africa and other lands were not being discovered. They were not lost. They were at home. It was the European pilgrims that were lost and who ended up in another people's home. Unfortunately, their mandated Doctrine of Discovery[4] had given them the license to pillage the people that they found on the basis of their difference.

---

4. Doctrine of Discovery: The papal bull issued by Pope Alexander VI on May 4, 1493, which played a central role in the Spanish conquest of the so-called "new world."

Thus we can see that this spirit of oppression around difference has deep roots in the psyches of those of European descent:
it should not be surprising that it requires deep, spiritually rooted
inner work to shift that determination to create categories of
superior and inferior persons. These categories require mainte-
nance by hierarchical structures to continue to foster separation
instead of community. There are times when it seems that there is
a DNA connection to the construct of white supremacy because
it pops its head into existence when least expected. It can be
difficult to name at times, such as when Anthony chided Wells
because Wells was willing to believe herself capable of deciding
how she wanted to live her life. When carefully reflecting upon
Anthony's rationale about why Wells should stay single, clearly
she is projecting Wells into the "extraordinary Negro" category,
making it necessary for her not to live as other women.

Catherine recalls the leaders of the little house church congregation trying to explain the need to avoid the Black Liberation
Struggle. How ludicrous was their reasoning. Ironically, they were
no older than was she and they did not know any better about
navigating through the pilgrim journey. But their whiteness and
their privilege gave them the distinct sense that they had a right
to speak about her liberation journey, a journey that they knew
nothing about and were not actively seeking to travel. How often
we disparage the "other" in ways that are the mere projections of
our imaginations.

In addition to the deep inner interrogation and reflection,
courage is critical to this process. It requires personal courage
that will not shrink from what one discovers in one's own heart.
This is true for black women as well as white women. For black
women, it is critical to have the courage to stand in their power
and accepting the responsibility to be faithful to the call to lead
in whatever way is presented to them. It takes courage to accept
without question the validity of their power because of the

internalized narratives of inferiority and denigration that must be excised.

The master narrative of white supremacy is so powerfully inscribed in every corner of the culture that it is impossible to avoid it in its totality. Even in cases such as Wells's where strong threads of resistance were planted in the soul by parents, one still has to navigate the larger world that spends most of its energy reinforcing the supremacy narrative and other black people who often find themselves helping to reinforce it. They do so by not resisting it as much as it needs to be resisted and at times inadvertently become complicit with it until they are awakened to what they are doing. Therefore, while black women have to resist the internalization of oppression, white women have to resist the narrative of superiority and the privilege that has grown out of that narrative.

The work of inner resistance to the narratives of white supremacy and internalized oppression would not be as complicated if we did not have the capacity to bury these narratives deeply in the unconscious. Often the efforts to forge new liberating narratives does not take into account that these old forms are deeply buried in the unconscious and that there is a fair amount of effort on the part of the ego to make sure that they stay safely buried.

As we embrace the work of understanding the intersection of gender and race, it is important to pay close attention to the shadow side of the equation. There is a clear and undeniable set-up between white women and black women that fuels the shadow or hidden side of each and supports projection. When one reflects upon the shadow as being the portion of the human psyche where unknown parts of the self reside with an enormous amount of potential for good and ill, it is helpful to explore that dynamic between black and white women.

White women, who were often placed on a patriarchal pedestal, looked as if they "had it all": The proverbial good life that the enslaved black women could not even imagine. This is a perfect set-up for black women to make up the imaginary white woman whose life is not nearly as it is in their imagination, but there is not any way to see that because they do not have a real relationship. On the other hand the white woman creates images of who the black woman is as well. Her imagination sees the all-caring, long-suffering, larger-than-life person who is so unlike she is and in many cases, the white woman joins in mistreating her. In spite of all of the peculiar dynamics between white women and their slaves, there was often a forbidden relationship that could easily be acknowledged. The relationship, whatever it happened to be, was subject to what white men named as being acceptable.

Projection is a psychological dynamic that arises out of individuals relating to others based upon their perceptions of them rather than who they happen to be and what makes them who they are. It is almost too much to take in when you really think about it in a clear fashion: two groups of people whose lives are intimately interwoven, yet they relate to one another as if the other is not really human. The daily interaction is dependent upon relating to made-up images. We see this with Anthony and Wells, as well as with Catherine's house church community. It is impossible to see the real person who stands in front of you when you have created them in whatever images your cultural narratives have taught you and in whatever ways your imagination has appropriated those narratives.

This is the reason that racial liberation has to embody more than simply deconstructing the indefensible systems that have been erected to support the white supremacy narrative. There is not any question that those systems have to be destroyed, but they will simply become the focus of great efforts of reconstruction if there is no work done to address the shadow and all of its energy for maintaining oppression. Earlier, the notion of personal courage as one of the tools for moving across the boundaries of the difficult intersection of race and gender was introduced. It is true that it takes much courage when the nature of the real liberation work is discovered. Too often, people will choose to retreat to the protection of the ego, which opts to maintain the status quo.

Resistance to the inner work can be engaged, but it cannot be justified by justice seeking people. Once the excavation begins in the unconscious, one loses the chance to stay safely rooted in the darkness. The light will go where it needs to go, if it is invited into the conversation. The feminist movement brought some light to the shadow between black and white women, but not enough. As thoughtful black women found ways not to settle for less light than was needed for deeper liberation to occur, the womanist movement was born in parts of Black America. This idea embodies a commitment to a holistic approach to liberation that includes black men, women, and children along with the environment. It is a more inclusive approach to liberation than was being offered to black women by the feminist process, which did not take into account that black women could not see the world as white women and that white women were a major part of the black woman's oppressing group. History had shown black women that when it came to the point of choosing struggles, white women would stand with white men instead of with black women and survival demanded that black women found their own path to liberation.

One of the places where this historical record was made quite clear was in the domestic worker and employer relationship. Black women were often called friend by the white women that they worked for, but the black woman knew that she had no place in which to stand and that she would not be defended against a white man if that need arose. The relationship was more like what one has with their treasured pet than with another person of equal value. Of course, there are a few exceptions where the black woman was deemed an exceptional human being and thus unlike every other black woman and more deserving of a higher place in the minds and hearts of the white woman and her family. Regardless of the rhetoric, the black woman was still the victim of projection and was never allowed to be an ordinary human being.

This reality was made very clear to Catherine at the funeral of a friend's mother who had been a domestic worker for many years for a white family. As those white family members spoke of her, they talked about how she was always at their house for holiday meals. Their conclusion was that she loved them so much that she wanted to be there to make sure that everything was perfect for them. There was never a single word spoken that demonstrated that they understood that she had left her family and that her little children did not have their mother with them until late in the day of the given holiday. The projection of her as loving them and being without any life that did not include serving them was phenomenal. But projection works both ways. So what does the black woman in this situation do in order to keep herself sane?

First, she is clear about the need to have the job that helps to take care of her family and keeping it is an essential duty. She divides herself to be the caring and long-suffering caretaker, she gets whatever material benefit she can from them, and she puts them in a place of importance in some corner of herself and closes the door. She learns how to keep that compartment separate from the rest of herself. She sees them far clearer than they see her. She is not there on holidays because she loves them; she is there because she has to be and she is not happy about it. But her starched and ironed face and clothing will never bear witness to what lies in her psyche. The white woman in the family is other and her life is perceived as easy because the black woman is her caretaker. She does the work and she bears the burdens that are passed onto her. She is much like the "mule of the world" as Hurston describes her. She is bearing all of the loads of whatever is brought to her and she is never seen as actually being present. She is merely the container for whatever is brought.

So back to the characterization of the black person as "beast" or "exceptional": the black woman becomes the "exceptional beast" who can bear all things and never flinch. This blindness does not disappear when one moves out of the slave and slave mistress or domestic and employer roles. The remnants of that mentality hang around the edges of the relationships black women and white women are attempting to forge and will prevent genuine ones from forming if the women involved do not wake up to the narratives that have helped to shape them.

Of course, twenty-first-century progressive white women will often stand to argue that they have managed to escape the narrative and are ready to embrace black women as equals and it rings true when the words are spoken. But, in this case and all others, actions speak much louder than words. When black women have power that must be acceded to, white women will often find themselves rethinking their progressive stance. When one finds it necessary to make the powerful black woman into some type of exceptional being instead of a mere human person who has embarked upon the pilgrim's journey of self-affirmation and authentication, there is a need for deep self-interrogation about the narratives that are being lived. When there is a temptation to explain the black woman's power or to create a narrative that makes her different from other black women, it is problematic for the relationship-building effort between white and black women.

Wells's experience with Anthony bears witness to Catherine's experience as the only black woman or as one of a few in professional settings: The projected image of exceptional was created to explain that presence. For Catherine, when a woman invited the other white women in the office to lunch in her presence, someone spoke up to ask if she would like to join them. The psychologist quickly chimed in, "We are going to the club and you cannot come because they do not allow blacks there." All of them left for lunch as though nothing strange had been said.

The invisible black woman without feelings was attached to Catherine and the small, inclusive acts in the daily run of working together all failed the major challenge of being "awake." So much in the same way that Susan B. Anthony fires her stenographer for acting in a racist manner toward Wells, but is not able to see Wells as an equal person, some of the women in this group tried to be cordial but got to their limitations quickly.

Another expression of the shadow projection is exhibited when there is too much praise for the work that is being done by black women. One is always appreciative of good work being acknowledged, but there is a point where there is no longer any reason to carry on about it. As a black woman, it is important not to become calloused and refuse to hear praise or criticism, but it is critical to psychological and spiritual health to keep a clearheaded perspective about all of it. The challenge for black women in this arena lies in not allowing the projections to become a part of their identity and not to project the white woman into being better than she actually happens to be.

The most important gift that one can be given is that of being seen as one truly happens to be and to be accepted on that basis. The dynamic of projection makes that impossible until it is recognized and addressed. One does not have to understand all of the particulars of the process in order to turn the energy around. Honest self-reflection is required, however, and the courage to allow the other person to be whomever they happen to be and to stay in the conversation until their personhood is acknowledged.

It is important to note that every human being engages in projection. And that those projections are made upon those

who are different from us and are deeply rooted in the unconscious and everything that has shaped that part of our psyche.
But the journey to self-liberation and wholeness requires the
challenging work of exploring the thoughts and feelings about
others and working to determine which ones exist only in our
hearts and heads and which ones have something to do with
the person to whom they are directed. Thus, black and white
women can certainly claim gender as a common denominator
and an important beginning point for the work of building
bridges, but there must be a serious commitment to allowing
each person to be encountered beyond their attributes and
faults. False comparisons cannot be made based solely on gender when race is equally as important to the liberation of black
women as is gender, an issue that white women do not have to
embrace unless they so choose.

This lengthy discussion regarding the shadow and the projections that emanate from it is important. It is challenging to
move beyond the desire for simple pathways to liberation. When
it comes to the race and gender intersection, it is critical to dig
into the foundation that supports the constructs that divide us
and to name those constructs. After naming them, the work of
deconstruction can begin, opening oneself to reconstructing a
new narrative that can actually support liberation. We are still a
good distance from true racial liberation and healing in our land
because we keep hoping that shortcuts will work.

We look for shortcuts in our religious communities and
we practice the nonsense of swapping pulpits and choirs, having a Wednesday night supper every three months, or marching
somewhere with a group of folks who will not be seen until the
next time a march is scheduled. In other communities we do the
same thing—white women asserting that all of us are together
because we share gender and the oppression of women, or that
we are together because we share interest in an issue such as

child welfare. All of these efforts refuse to address the narrative of white supremacy that stands at the pathway of all other forms of oppression. Until that acknowledgment is made in a clear and unequivocal manner, no sustainable racial healing will occur.

Our current situation bears witness to the truth of this assertion. We are watching voter suppression in the 2018 election cycle reminiscent of the atmosphere of the 1950s. The current assaults on blacks and other people of color seem almost surreal. While it is tempting to think that a new energy system is emerging in the land making all of this possible, that is not the case. It is energy that has always been present, hidden in the deep recesses of our unconscious.

In a very important way it is the best of times for those who are seeking to be truly liberated because these times make hiding impossible. The truth seekers have to stand up to be counted. The projections have to be replaced with reality, creating the brave space where a new narrative can be born. This is the path to salvation: the withdrawing of a false reality projected into the world as authentic and replacing it with the truth. Brave spaces must be created where the truth can be spoken and heard. The false images have to die. They will not die easily, and clearly this period in our history bears witness to the pain of the death of false ways of seeing. The white supremacy narrative created a false reality and it has to die. It is dying, and one of these days it will be replaced with a new narrative of inclusion for all of God's children as equal humans on this earth.

Though that day is not here yet, one of the most important spaces where true racial healing work can be done is in the spaces where genuine community is forged. Ida B. Wells knew that black women had to create such communities for their survival because they could not wait for white women to open liberation's door. Thus, she was very involved in the "Negro Women's Club Movement" in the late 1890s and was a major influence in their growth. She served as president of the Ida B. Wells Club, which was founded in her honor. Even though she was one of the more popular figures in this movement, she was clear about the need to stand against ideas of respectability and refinement when that stance required sacrificing the truth about lynching and the other assaults upon the integrity of black life. This position caused conflict between Wells and Mary Church Terrell and others who espoused respectability and refinement as a major place to hold, but she continued to maintain her position that woman suffrage and racial uplift did not get separated as the primary core issue for black people.

She supported the process that led to the founding of the National Association for the Advancement of Colored People. She did so because she understood that the formation of as many forms of alliances as possible within the race were needed to support the crucial liberation efforts that black people had to engage. Unfortunately, the sexism of Du Bois and others kept her from being a part of the leadership as would have been fitting considering that she had played a major role in its founding. In spite of the conflicts between Wells and her counterparts, both men and women, she managed to keep a clear-eyed focus upon the work and never allowed herself to veer off the course of fighting against lynching and for the rights of women.

Ida B. Wells's dogged adherence to the mission of antilynching work and fighting for woman's suffrage along with overall liberation for black people serves as an amazing model for us in the twenty-first century. We have allowed ourselves to be kidnapped by the illusion of liberation because a few laws got overturned and we gained access to a bit of delegated white power. That illusion has caused us to allow ourselves to be less compassionate than we need to be toward those in our own communities who are poor, imprisoned, and who find themselves unable to navigate the path of life in ways that are supportive of finding the best for themselves. It has led in too many cases to a harshness that is very unfortunate and unbecoming of a people who share a legacy of slavery, lynching, Jim Crow, and twenty-first-century efforts to reassert white supremacy as it is challenged by the loss of its majority status. The illusion of liberation has to be placed in conversation with the reality of all black people and not simply the handful allowed to experience the luxury of delegated white power such as politicians, police, and corporate leaders. This illusory liberation has served to create a state of amnesia in too many corners of our community and allows too many to act as if the liberation struggle has been won.

Wells, especially after her marriage to Attorney Ferdinand Lee Barnett, could have chosen to remove herself from the struggle against lynching and all of the other demons of oppression that she tackled to follow the respectability and refinement path, but she did not. It appears that she did not because her call to the work was a genuine vocational call that would not have allowed her to do anything else.

This moment in America offers a similar choice to those who have been fortunate enough to gain a place of stability and choice. Wells challenges all of us who know of her even in the most cursory manner to reflect upon what the answer needs to be for us. While the call is to everyone, I think that we women may need to rethink where we are in this current conversation. It is clear that many white women are opting to follow the historical path of supporting the men and more progressive white women are going to the mat for issues confronting women. Thus, black women have to do the critical work that was described so eloquently by Zora Neale Hurston's character Janie as she describes letting go of the projection of her second husband, "Something fell off the shelf inside of me, and I went in there to look and found that it was my image of Jody. I knew then that I had an inside and outside and that I would never let them be mixed up."[5] It is this type of clarity in the depths of one's soul that can lead to finding the answer for the call on one's life.

While this is not an argument about women having more responsibility than men, it is a statement about women taking the time not to behave in the same manner as men. It is an attempt to engage in a conversation that is asking how does the power of women, especially black women, differ from that of men? How will women use their power in ways that bring the whole race forward and not simply benefit their particular personal agenda? Can women finally define power for themselves? Can women find the courage to imagine power as something new and different from the ways in which it has been forged by men? The time has come and gone for women to simply behave as if they are inferior men. Wells and many of the pioneers of that era dared to be different. They dared to define their way to be in the world. Wells began that process as a young sixteen-year-old girl when she took on the care of her young siblings at the death of her parents; she lived on the terms that her heart and head demanded. It is not extraordinary for a person to live like Ida B. Wells so it can happen in any era. It requires listening to the music of a different drummer and having the courage to march to that music. Sometimes it is possible to hear the music, but it takes personal courage to march because then others see what you are doing. It is in the marching that one gets labeled when choices move beyond respectability and refinement in the work for racial and gender equality.

Since the early 1900s the black community has had the benefit of the Greek Letter organizations that continue to thrive in this moment and that were founded upon the premise of helping to create a more equitable community for black people. Most of them have service as a core portion of their mission. Both the

---

5. Zora Neale Hurston, *Their Eyes Were Watching God* (New York: Harper Perennial Modern Classics, 2006), 186.

fraternities and sororities have a major role to play and while they do much good in the communities, it is time for a new infusion of commitment and intentional energy to be turned toward the challenges that face the African American community.

The black women's clubs and later the Greek Letter groups were organized because it was clear that the answer to the struggles in the community had to be taken up by black people who would form alliances with whites who wanted to be liberated in order to make the world better for black people in general. It continues to be true and as was true with the civil rights movement, women took the lead in it. If they had not, there would not have been a movement. Black women will have to do that again. They can build alliances with white women who want to be liberated and who are more interested in being well than being white, but they must take the lead.

While we happily celebrate the infusion of many new black and white female faces in the 2018 election cycle, it is important not to get too happy too quickly. The women, who are bound to be elected because the numbers will assure that, must redefine power and how they use it. If that does not happen, then the struggle for genuine healing around race, gender, and class will not occur. While it is critical not to be caught in hoping for female saviors to come onto the scene, it is important to work to create the new conversations that are being suggested in these words. The conversation of this current era of repression and oppression has to be silenced and replaced with one of liberation and a new understanding of power, which can be derived from reimagining this country as a place where healing is possible and deeply desired.

It is important to ask whether or not we can imagine an America where we allow everyone to be an equal member of the society. Perhaps the foundation of white supremacy has rendered us helpless in turning ourselves around. Many have imagined this land to be a place where many folks have to be at the bottom while they think it is their place to be above and in control of them. This imagination has a hold on all of us, but it is losing its efficacy because it is not defensible and human beings were not created to be in bondage. It is not the way of the Creator to have a land of people in bondage, though human beings have been doing this to one another for a long time. Its life cycle is threatened more in this present moment than ever before. This threat to the indefensible system of white supremacy and all of its offspring accounts for much of the fragmentation, violence, and fear that we see now.

Wells would caution us to hold onto our faith. She would chastise us. Those of us in the present day have such a great legacy upon which to call as we seek to forge the path to authentic liberation. What can be the reason for not acting courageously? How can we settle for the illusion of freedom when true freedom is possible? How can we live around the edges of liberation while confronting the daily assaults of microaggressions from an ambivalent white world when more liberation is possible? How can we be satisfied in our gated communities with their pseudo sense of security when our sisters and brothers sleep under bridges and in prisons where there is no security? We are standing at the crossroads and they are asking which way do we want to go? Unlike illiterate Sojourner Truth who was destined to go whichever way the mules took her since she could not read the road signs, we can read the signs, but we desperately need her humility of spirit. The spirit that was willing to let go of the mule lines and allow God to send her wherever she needed to go. Wells, Truth, and so many others are standing at our crossroads asking us, What are we planning to do?

This chapter has spent a bit of time arguing for ordinary human beings who are at the crossroads and simply trying to hold on to being human. There are no beasts here and there are no extraordinary people—just frail, strong, courageous, cowardly, wounded, healthy, wise, foolish, well, ill, fearful, brave human beings; just humans who are standing at the crossroads with all of those traits listed and many others, but with the great capability to reframe the narratives. That capacity to reframe their imagination and that of the country is crucial. The possibility of America is in front of these ordinary human persons who can be empowered just as those ancestors who have come and gone. No, they are not beasts and they are not extraordinary. They struggle and they want to rest more than they want to be revolutionaries. They had hoped that the struggle was over and the jolt of the reality that it is far from over is a struggle within itself. But they remember their heritage and how many have given everything that they had to make America be the America that was being imagined for whites only. They believe the vision of a place where liberty can live is possible.

Wells is still speaking in a voice that is more powerful than ever. She held the paradoxes in her hands and her heart. She lived in that world of affluence and never let herself forget those with nothing. She had a chance to be the secure wife of Barnett and she kept speaking about lynching and putting herself in harm's way. She kept writing, so she is waiting for us. She reminds us that we are the ones that we are looking to find. There are no others. We have a great cloud of witnesses, but they are not coming back to do the work and there is much yet to do. We stand in the midst of the intersections of race and gender and many other manifestations of oppression, and we have the opportunity to start the liberating conversations. Wells marches on with us and watches to see how we will frame the conversations that will support the legacy that she and so many others forged for us.

The acceptance of Wells as someone who was simply trying to be human and who went about living in a manner that bore witness to that possibility for many others helps us not to project her into heroine status so that she becomes less of a challenge. If she is a simple ordinary woman who struggled with common human issues and managed to be this giant from whom we continue to take counsel, then perhaps there is a possibility that there is a similar call for us.

Therefore, it seems imperative to honor her by listening as Dr. Howard Thurman would caution us to do, "for the sound of the genuine" for ourselves and to heed that call. Wells would be glad to know that her legacy moved folks in the twenty-first century to do that.

Questions for Further Reflection

1. Do you see Wells as an ordinary woman or a very extraordinary person? Why?
2. What is your response to the concept of invisibility blues? Do you have any experiences that help you to understand this concept?
3. Do you think that the power that women have is the same as it is for men or not? If not, what makes it different? If it is the same, reflect upon what has led you to this particular perspective.
4. How do you see white women and black women building bridges to one another?

CHAPTER 6

"Order Our Steps"

Nibs writes as a person classified as "white" to suggest seven steps that will enable those of us classified as "white" to begin to acknowledge our captivity to race and to begin to seek some liberation from that captivity.

I use the phrase "classified as white" to indicate that racial categories are political constructs, that there is no basis for race in biology or genetics or even culture. While there is great diversity in the human family, the system of race is not designed to denote and to affirm that diversity. Instead, it is designed to assert who should have power and who should be in control: those classified as "white."

As those of us classified as "white" seek to move toward a recovery of our own humanity, let us be guided by these steps: recognition, repentance, resistance, resilience, reparations, reconciliation, and recovery. Many of us classified as "white" want to begin with reconciliation as step one or two, but that is because we misunderstand the depth of our captivity. We must have some steps of liberation before we can even think about reconciliation. Though these seven steps are useful for other kinds of captivity and are useful for those who are not classified as "white," they are meant primarily for those of us classified as "white."

In using these seven steps, I am using the model of "addiction" as a primary one in reference to white people being captive to the power of race. There are many other models that have been used, but from my point of view, addiction is a very helpful one. In this sense, all of us who are classified as "white" will always be "recovering racists." To some this may sound harsh, but my experience in engaging white folks on the issue of race has made me move toward this helpful model. These steps—recognition, repentance, resistance, resilience, reparations, reconciliation, and recovery—are not linear—they are more like a spiral, where we will continue to revisit all of them at various stages in our lives.

A recent example may help us to understand the depth of our captivity. I gave a lecture at Princeton Seminary in the summer of 2018 at the Karl Barth Pastors Conference. In that lecture, I suggested that Barth had needed to emphasize the power of the neighbor as one of the primary sources of revelation from God. I used my story and the power of race in my life and in the life of American culture as primary examples of God's sending the neighbor to us to help us understand the depth of our captivity to sin as human beings.

After the lecture a middle-aged white man from Canada came up to talk with me. He indicated that he did not grow up in the white, racist culture of the American South, and because of that, he was not sure that my examples applied to him or to Canadians. I responded that some of the best writings and descriptions of encounters with race that I had heard came from First Nations peoples of Canada. He then proceeded to tell me that one of his best friends was a person of native origin, and their friendship was evidence that he himself was not captured by race. I replied that I had heard such disclaimers all of my adult life in America whenever a white person was confronted by the power of race in their lives. I then asked about the issues of the land in Canada and the need for reparations there. He replied again that he thought that was a complicated issue, but that in the end, "God owns the land." I asked him if he had deeds to some of the land, and he replied that he did. I said, "If God owns the land, why not give your deed to the church or some nonprofit mission group to be used for God's work?" His reply was: "I'm tired of feeling guilty about this kind of stuff." I urged him: "Then open your eyes and your heart to recognize your captivity and see where God takes you on this." He went away after that, but I hope that he begins to explore the step of recognition.

In August 2015 I was listening to NPR's "Fresh Air," hosted by Terri Gross. On the program that day was Larry Wilmore, an African American comic who had just hosted the hundredth episode of his show on Comedy Central, filling in the old Steven Colbert slot. She commended him for his success and also commended him for incorporating "race" into his show, adding "race is the most difficult subject to talk about in America."[1]

I wish that Wilmore had interrupted his interviewer right there, and asked: "You know, Terri, why is race so difficult to talk about in America? Why is it so hard to talk about something with such obvious power in American history and in current American culture?" It had tremendous power in Ida Wells's life. Although we have made some progress in diminishing its power from that time, race has "shape-shifted" and has taken on new forms. Currently, race is seeking to return to its power of the time of Ida Wells.

Why is race so difficult to discuss and engage in America? We must face that question and its answer, especially those of us classified as "white." It is so difficult to talk about race in America because we who are white continue to want to deny its power in our own individual and structural and institutional lives. We are not ready to go there—we can't quite get there. We

---

1. "With 100th Episode, Larry Wilmore's 'Nightly Show' Has Found Its Voice," NPR, August 19, 2015, *https://www.npr.org/templates/transcript/transcript.php?storyId=432906983.*

can't acknowledge how deeply "race" is embedded in our lives, in our imaginations, and in our institutions. Because of this, the conversations and engagements on race are difficult for all of us in America. Such a topic also calls into question the narrative of America—born in innocence, developed out of sheer willpower and hard work, driven by the ideology that all people are created equal. In order to make any progress on race in America, we will have to engage those stories of national origin and find the complexity and contradictions in their development.

The power of whiteness does not pertain only to those classified as "white." It works to tell white folks that we are superior, but it also works to tell all others that they are inferior. My purpose here is to lift the lid off the box of whiteness and race in our individual and communal and cultural lives—to allow some air in—so that we can first acknowledge the depth of the power of race in our lives. Then, we can begin to find ways to engage its power in our individual lives, in our institutional lives, and in the life of America. The recent shootings of black people by police officers, revealed on social media, are not new occurrences—what is new is that they have been revealed to larger and whiter audiences. Even the white Millenials, who have generally discounted the power of race in their individual and communal lives, are beginning to pay attention. I must say at this point that I am not hopeful that this conversation and engagement will make much difference, but I will be delighted to be wrong. The Black Lives Matter Movement gives me some hope. I am also inspired by the witness of Ida Wells, who never gave up on the fight for justice, and who always expected that justice would be forthcoming.

In regard to race, in order to move toward life, we must have *recognition*. Recognition is the first step for those of us who are classified as "white." For many years now I have been fascinated by Mary Magdalene's encounter with the risen Jesus in the graveyard in John 20. The risen Jesus is standing in front of her, and they are in conversation with one another, but she does not recognize him as the risen Jesus—she thinks that he is the cemetery's caretaker. I am intrigued that she cannot recognize him—why not? She has traveled with him as a colleague in ministry for three years, and Luke 8 tells us that he healed her of mental illness. She knows this guy—why can't she recognize him? It's not that he looks weird, like a ghost or a zombie—she thinks that he is a human being, just not Jesus. My answer is that she is captured by the power of death—she is not looking for a living Jesus—she is looking for a dead body. Her perceptual apparatus is not able to see that he is the friend who has been executed by the Roman Empire. The power of empire and death have captured her heart and her mind and her spirit—she is simply not able to recognize the risen Jesus.

Most of us who are classified as "white" are unable to recognize our captivity to race. Recognition of the continuing power of race in our lives is an essential first step for those of us classified as "white." It is a system "by us, for us," to paraphrase and reverse "FUBU," the African American clothing line whose "for us, by us" became a central marketing tag. Much of the difficulty of engaging the power of race in our individual lives and in our collective lives is rooted in the fundamental resistance, even denial, that we have in acknowledging how deeply embedded race is in our lives. In a previous book, I have designated this process as "the system of race."[2]

A second part of this recognition is the realization that all of us have been taught this system of race by people who love us. As a white boy growing up in the segregated South, I was taught this system by good white people who believed that white supremacy

---

2. Nibs Stroupe and Inez Fleming, *While We Run This Race* (Maryknoll, NY: Orbis Books, 1995), 21.

was God's will. To use the provocative phrase from Ephesians 2:1–2, I came under the power of death through "the prince of the power of the air." In what often happens in my encounters with the Bible, what seems at first to be such a primitive approach turns out to be sophisticated and always modern. The very air that we need to have life also brings us pollutants that bring us death. So it is with the system of race. The very folks who nurtured me and loved me and brought me life also taught me the power of white supremacy. Whenever we talk about the stuff of recognition in regard to race and white supremacy, we must always remember that we breathed it in, that it permeates much of our being, just as the oxygen from our breath goes all through our bodies. The stuff of recognition in regard to race is not so much moving from being bad to being good—it is rather about seeing ourselves and others in a whole new way. In saying this, I am not dismissing the barbarity of the system of race— rather, I am reminding us that it is interwoven with our being, and that it will be a struggle to begin to move toward liberation from the depths of its power. We underestimate its power at our peril and at the peril of so many others.

Mary did come to recognize the risen Jesus—how did it happen? He called her name: "Mary." And she ran to tell the other disciples: "I have seen the Lord!" So let it be with us. Let us go to those places where death seems to have reign, as Mary did, and there, if we are blessed, maybe we too will hear our name called, and we too can begin to have the shackles of race removed from our hearts, and we too can begin to move from seeing the dead white Christ and move toward the vibrant and life-giving black Jesus. This is how it works in my life.

I remember the phone call well. It came to the church office about two years into our ministry at Oakhurst. It came from one of our African American elders. She had called me because she had a concern about a decision that I had made as pastor, and although I can remember seeing myself sitting at my desk in the office, I do not remember the issue that she wanted to address. As we talked and discussed and obviously disagreed on the decision, I asked her why she was so angry about this decision. She surprised me with her reply: "What makes you think that I am angry?" I thought that it was obvious, so I answered: "You sound mad." She said: "No, I'm not angry—believe me, if I was angry, you would know it, there would be no doubt about it. No, I'm not angry."

There was a silence after that—I wasn't sure what to say. So she stepped into the silence: "I'm not angry, but I am interested that you thought that I was angry about this. It is intriguing, and I think that I have an answer, but I don't know that you are willing to hear it. Are you willing to receive this?" Another long silence, as I mulled my options. "OK, let's hear it," I said, feeling both irritated and anxious. "I'm guessing that you as a white man in power are not accustomed to having a black person treat you as a peer, that you are not accustomed to having black women stand up to you. My treating you as an equal is something that makes you angry and instead of owning up to that, you projected your anger onto me. Is that right? How does that sound?" Another long silence—it seemed like five minutes to me, but I'm guessing that it was about thirty seconds. She had indeed interpreted my feelings, although I wanted to add that as pastor, I should be in charge. I had a moment of revelation then, and I responded, hesitantly, "Yes, I think that you may be right. I am in uncharted territory here." I expected the wrath of God to come down on me because my racism was exposed, but she stunned me again when she replied: "Now, we can work with this. As long as I know that you know, and that you will occasionally acknowledge your racism, we can work together. You may be surprised at your racism, but I am not, and none of the black people at Oakhurst are surprised either." It was a moment of recognition, and we went on to become allies and friends, and to write the book on racism together.

I was blessed to have an African American person who was willing to engage me and my racism, and I give thanks for that. I want to emphasize, however, that going on this seven-step journey is my responsibility. It is not the responsibility of people of color to engage me or change me—that responsibility belongs to me and to all of us who are classified as "white." And I cannot say it often enough—all of us who are classified as "white" are captive to this power, are addicted to this power, and we must all go on this journey in some form or fashion. Our denial of this deadly power is what leads to death for us and to death for so many others. Our souls die. Ida Wells experienced this denial in the deadly scourge of lynchings. We continue to see it in the police shootings of people of color in mass incarceration, as well as in the daily erosion of the spirits and lives of so many people of color who are consigned to the margins of society and life.

As the biblical witness indicates, blessed are we if God intercedes in our captivity and begins to give us the stuff of recognition so that, like Mary Magdalene, we can begin to see the risen Jesus standing right in front of us. It is a conversion, a recognition that will take us into new places in ourselves and in the world. It is an experience that will begin to change our perceptual apparatus, which will begin to help us see others and ourselves in a whole new light.

After this first step of recognition comes the second step of *repentance*. When I first began to work on this list of steps to enable us to engage the continuing power of race in our lies, I heard from a colleague and friend, Dr. Chris Boesel, who teaches at Drew School of Theology. He urged me to consider adding "repentance" to the list. I had given this some consideration when I devised the list of "R" words, but I had decided to leave it out because of the connotations that it has in American Christianity, especially Southern white Christianity. In our individualistic slaveholders-captivity-of-the-Gospel context, it has come to mean "to stop doing bad things," and it puts too much trust in the human will. Yet here I am adding it in, in honor of Ida Wells (and thanks to the push of Chris Boesel). Wells and her contemporaries and generations after her had to go through so much pain and struggle because of racism. Those of us who are classified as "white" must come to terms with the pain that we have caused and continue to cause. After recognizing that need, we must then move to the step of repentance.

When Jesus proclaims in Mark 1:15 that the time is at hand and that the Beloved Community is near, he tells us to "repent and believe the good news!" It took me awhile in my journey to hear that "repent" not only meant changing our actions but also transforming our imaginations and our perceptual apparatus so that we see a whole new world. In the context of the system of race, it asks all of us, but especially those of us classified as white, to see our own humanity and those of others in a new way. For most of us, this sounds like one more piece of "oughtness," one more thing that we have to do. Yet in his proclamation, Jesus tells us that it is good news. The idea of repentance, especially in regard to race, asks us to consider that the system of race is one of those "fake news items," designed to throw us off the mark and separate us from ourselves and from one another.

My experience is that once we begin this journey, it will be a long, stumbling, bumbling journey because of our captivity to race and to many other powers. "Repentance," then, is rarely a one-time event but is part of a journey with many sideways steps. Another Gospel encounter reflects this experience with repentance. In Luke 5, Peter the fisherman engages Jesus, but in a way that he had never imagined.

Jesus comes to Peter after Peter has had a long and frustrating night of catching no fish. Because Jesus's presence and message is so powerful, folks are flocking to him to seek repentance and healing and a new vision of God and of life. Jesus asks Peter to let him come into the boat and then take him out a bit into the lake, so that he will have some space to teach and preach. Peter has already experienced Jesus's power in the healing of his own mother-in-law, so even though he is tired and frustrated, he accommodates Jesus. After Jesus finishes teaching the crowd, he tells Peter to go further out into the deeper waters in order to catch some fish. Peter responds from his human point of view: "Teacher, we've been out there all night—there are no fish available." How can this preacher know anything about fishing? Yet because he is grateful to Jesus for healing his mother-in-law, he again accommodates Jesus, and he goes out into the deeper waters.

The result is stunning—the nets fill with fish. Rather than shouting "Hallelujah! Thank you, Jesus," Peter tells Jesus to get away from him. He tells Jesus to get away from him because he has just seen that Jesus will require him to go out into the deeper waters of repentance and renewal. He won't be able to stay in his comfort zone—he will be asked to see himself and life differently. I have experienced this myself and have watched others experience it in regard to race. Jesus comes to us and demonstrates a new power of vitality and life and a new way of seeing the world, and we are required to make a decision about this engagement. Many of us who are classified as white often recognize that saying "yes" to Jesus will not only take us into deeper waters—it will begin to change our lives. This is where repentance comes in. If we say "yes" to Jesus, we won't be able to go back to our white world in quite the same way. Many of us say "no" to Jesus, and that is why racism remains so strong in our time. We do not want to go into those deeper waters, even though there is great promise in doing so. To repent, to say "yes" to Jesus, will take us into unchartered territory, where the world of race that we have received—and have helped to build—will begin to change.

This change will be similar to what Peter experienced on that boat on Gennesaret Lake—he will perceive realities that he had completely missed before. "Look, Teacher, we have been out on those waters all night, and there are no fish out there." Peter knows how the world works, and Jesus does not. Yet Peter says "yes," and the landscape changes for him. In the days and months and years to come in Peter's life, he will not be forcing himself to perceive the world differently—it will be changing before his eyes, as it did on that day on Gennesaret. This is the root meaning of repentance, and it is a necessary step on the road to engaging racism. We who are classified as white are asked to listen to Jesus, to hear that the world of our mothers and fathers and colleagues— the world of race and captivity and domination—is not the only reality. In fact, it is a demonic reality that sucks the life and wind and joy out of us. Our current time shows us that it is very powerful "fake news."

We are captive to this "fake news," and Peter's journey is both good news for us and a sobering reminder of our captivity. Though he has a very powerful repentance in those deeper waters, his journey into liberation is steep and stumbling. He seems always to be messing up, and yet Jesus is always redeeming him and continuing to transform him. Jesus does this because he does not want Peter's perfection. He wants his passion, and that is at the heart of the idea of repentance. Peter begins to see himself and the world differently, and his passion moves from the anxieties of his life to the love of his life. He remains captive to the powers until he disappears from the biblical story after his conversion on the Gentiles in Acts 10–12, but he is remembered as the leader of the church after the Ascension of Jesus.

So, yes, repentance is a necessary step in this journey with Jesus, taking a step out of the land of race toward the Beloved Community. It remains a struggle, but I have a vision of it, and I have made a commitment to this new vision. It means that all of us (and I do mean "all of us") who are classified as "white" must remember that we are always recovering racists.

I don't know if Ida Wells had much hope for white people or not. I do know that she was a fierce fighter for justice, and part of her determination was her discovery of the depth of resistance in white supremacy. In return, she was a committed resistance fighter. The third step, *resistance*, speaks of both the power of our captivity and the need for our commitment to the new world revealed in recognition and repentance. Throughout the history of the European presence in America, there has been African American, Native American, Hispanic, and Asian resistance to white supremacy. People have risen up in resistance, both violent and nonviolent, to the idea that white supremacy is the natural order and is God's intention. Ida Wells was one of the primary resisters of this idea of white supremacy. Her entire life was one of resistance: on the train from Memphis in 1884, in her articles on lynching in the 1890s, in her trips to Britain to raise consciousness and funding for the antilynching movement, in refusing to take a backseat to black male leadership, in her refusal to allow the white suffragists to keep her out of the 1913 parade, in her confrontation with newly elected President Woodrow Wilson, in her urging the Arkansas men to resist their unjust death sentences, and in so many other instances.

This idea of resistance has at least three levels. We must start with the truth that people classified as "nonwhite" have been resisting this demonic power of racial classification for centuries, understanding very well that the purpose of the system of race is not to classify the diverse family of humanity but rather to justify the hoarding of power and resources for those classified as "white." This level is part of the step of recognition, but it must be repeated here because it is so important and so pervasive. All of us classified as "white" resist the idea that we, or our institutions, are captured by the power of race. "There might be other white people who are racists, but not me. I don't see color," is often how the conversation moves. As my friend David Billings has put it in his fine book: we who are "white" are in "deep denial."[3] We strongly resist the truth that white privilege exists, and that it greatly benefits us.

We must acknowledge how resistant we are to admitting our captivity to race. We resist it because it belies our national origin stories of individualism and meritocracy and endless opportunity. We resist it because we believe that God has ordained white supremacy. Thus, this third step of resistance recognizes how difficult it will be to acknowledge our captivity and to begin to seek some liberation from it, both individually and collectively.

Even if we who are white are able to admit this truth, we find it difficult to lessen its power over us and in us. This leads us to the third level of resistance, as we seek to turn this power around and begin to use it to regain our humanity rather than using it to diminish our humanity. We must begin to resist the power of race in our lives as individuals and as communities. It will be a powerful struggle in our souls and in our institutions. It will feel like Paul's admonition to himself in Romans 7:14–25, where he describes himself as being at war with himself, as he seeks to live as a child of God. He wants to live as God's child but often finds himself obeying the call of the powers of the world. I have experienced this many times in my own life, and one instance leaps out at me from twenty years ago, as I rode the subway into downtown Atlanta. At a stop in the black neighborhood, several young African American males got on the train, joking and clowning and speaking loudly. I noticed a bit of tension beginning to build in myself. At the same time, I noticed that someone had gotten on the train and sat behind me. This person was reeking of alcohol, and I found myself putting these two occurrences

---

3. Billings, *Deep Denial*.

together. I thought to myself, "Black males really need to get their act together—they shouldn't be dissipating their lives in this manner." I pondered these things and solutions to them as we rode on the train together, knowing that I was the only white person in that train car. Then, a couple of stops later, the man behind me, who had been reeking of alcohol, got up and exited the train—he was a well-dressed white man. My racism was exposed to myself, and I echoed Paul's words in Romans 7:24: "Wretched man that I am! Who will rescue me from this body of death?"

That was one of the many consciousness-raising experiences that I was blessed to have in the thirty years at Oakhurst Presbyterian Church. Yet the power of race remains in me—not as strong, but still traces of it. I cannot seem to scour it out, and this idea of continuing the work of resistance resonates strongly in me. Why is it so deep in me and in so many of us classified as "white"? Two metaphors have emerged that have been helpful to me: demonic possession and addiction. Our modern ears recoil at the idea of demonic possession, an idea that has been used so often to harm many people, especially in the church. Yet it seems to describe the captivity to racism with which so many of us who are white are afflicted. I described this earlier in more detail.

The second metaphor is that of addiction—we who are classified as white are addicted to it. Just as addicts will do many strange things and will remain in deep denial about their addiction, so it is with many of us who cling to "whiteness" as one of our primary identities. Our addiction allows us to hold on to a certain view of the world, a view that is destructive to ourselves and to others, but a view that we maintain as strongly as we can. The key steps in dealing with addiction is to come out of denial and find a community of support. These steps are part of the process in moving toward healing our captivity to race as "white" people.

Both of these metaphors point to the depths of our captivity to race, and they both call out to us for the need for movement on our parts: coming out of denial and seeking community support. They also point to a fundamental truth about this third step on the road to recovery. The power of race is highly resistant to change, and thus we must be ready to acknowledge our captivity and to be ready to resist the wiles of the demonic and addictive power of race. This is no journey for the faint-hearted—it requires courage and discipline, and endurance. Yet as Jesus once taught us, one of our great assets will be to develop the quality of the fourth step on the road to recovery: *resilience.*

Like any deeply rooted system, the power of race is both resistant and resilient in response to the few attempts to mitigate its power. In the 1870s and 1880s, the white Southern powers began developing a two pronged and resilient approach to reestablish slavery. They used both violence and legislation, knowing that they could not overtly indicate that they were working to reestablish slavery. In the 1890s they adopted what came to be known as the "Mississippi Plan," a coordination of violence and legislation that sought to intimidate and restrict black rights and movement (and white sympathizers), never mentioning the word "race" or "racism." They bet that the federal government and the Supreme Court would accept their premise that in the world of race, intent was more important than results. They were correct—in several decisions in the 1890s, the Supreme Court upheld neo-slavery because no intent to reestablish slavery or to develop systems based on race was expressed in the laws that were reviewed. This distinction between intent and result is an essential tool in the white power work to preserve our current system of race. In October 2018, the US Supreme Court voted 5–4 to uphold a North Dakota state law that disenfranchised Native American voters. The North Dakota law required that all voters have a street address, and those North Dakotans who lived on reservations all had post office boxes. No intent to discriminate based on race was expressed, but its purpose was clear—take the vote away from as many Native Americans as possible.[4]

Ida Wells was raised to hear that she was a child of God, even when she was born in slavery. She expressed that reality and that expectation when she sued the Chesapeake and Ohio Railroad for kicking her off the train in 1884 because she refused to be forced to go to the segregated train car. In 1887, when the Tennessee Supreme Court overturned her initial court victory, she was despondent and faced a fundamental decision. She could have decided to accept her defeat and resign herself to the power of racism and get by as best she could. Showing the resilience that was one of her trademarks, Ida Wells did not resign herself—she chose to continue the fight for justice and equality, and indeed she only grew in her resistance. Like the founders of Black Lives Matter, she decided to step up the fight, rather than stepping back. Though she and I are coming from different ends of the spectrum—hers was an engagement with internalized inferiority; mine an engagement with internalized superiority—her remarkable resilience is the foundation for my fourth step that those classified as "white" must engage and must work: resilience.

When Barack Obama was elected as the 44th and first African American president, some people saw it as evidence that the power of racism had diminished. Perhaps it is my white Southern heritage, but even though I hoped that sentiment was true, I knew that it was not. Throughout the history of this country, white folks have emphasized so strongly that race is just about over. The election of an African American president prompted the idea among white people that we are now in a postracial society, but it also triggered that deeply held white belief that black people cannot handle

---

4. *Brakebill v. Jaeger*. Tal Axelrod, "Native American Tribe Slams Supreme Court Decision Upholding North Dakota Voter ID Law," The Hill, October 11, 2018, *https://thehill.com/homenews/state-watch/411085-native-american-tribe-slams-supreme-court-decision-upholding-north*.

political power—hence the almost constant NO in response to President Obama as a person and as president. The rise of the Tea Party is the resonating voice of the Mississippi Plan of the 1890s, and we continue to see this river of racism, resistance, and resilience that is flowing ever more strongly in the open waters of American society. In her 2016 book *White Rage*, Dr. Carol Anderson gives a running history of this white response to the movements for justice and equality.[5] The extralegal lynchings have been replaced by the targeting of African Americans and Latinx by the police and the court system. The development of social media has recorded this state-sanctioned violence, and even then, there is still strong white denial that this is the power of race and not the criminal tendencies of African American and Latinx people.

We who are classified as "white" have noted that there may be some lingering injustices that seem racially based, but we have often dismissed those as part of the clean-up operation or as the responsibility of those being oppressed. I experienced this in a surprising way in 1993, when I sent a manuscript on the power of race in American life to the publisher of my first book *While We Run This Race*. They were interested in it, but some of their consultants felt that it emphasized race way too much. I remember a telephone conversation with our editor, who told me that they felt that the power of race was just about over, that class was the biggest problem now in American society. I was shocked to hear this, but I wanted to get this book published. As a compromise, I agreed that I would delete most of the historical work in the manuscript that compared post-Reconstruction to the 1980s and early 1990s.[6]

I share that story to indicate that the power of race in American culture is both persistent and resilient. In 2018 we are all

---

5. Carol Anderson, *White Rage* (New York: Bloomsbury Publishing, 2016).

6. Letter from Robert Ellsberg to Nibs Stroupe, January 24, 1994.

now well aware of how powerful it is, because of the social media exposure of police brutality and killings of black and Latino people. In 2018 in Georgia, we saw evidence of this resilient power of race. A rural county in southwest Georgia proposed closing seven of its nine polling places, ostensibly because they were not ADA compliant. The real reason: in a majority black county, a white consultant, who was a colleague of the white gubernatorial candidate, saw this as a way of blunting black political power, which might help elect the black opponent in the governor's race.[7]

Let us never lose sight of the power of race in American society. In order to combat it, we will need to be resilient ourselves. The teenager Mary of Nazareth hears a request from God to put herself in peril and to swim against the stream of oppression by allowing herself to be the mother of Jesus, who will live at the margins of society. She asks, "How is this possible?" The answer that she hears in Luke 1 is a reminder that God has come and is coming to help us hear about the power of another story, a story that moves us away from the oppressive systems of race and gender and class and militarism toward the systems of justice and love and equity. She hears that she must be resilient in this journey, and once she agrees, she goes first not to her fiancé, Joseph, but to her cousin Elizabeth. In finding solidarity there with her womanist community, she is able to face and endure the resilient power and resistance to equity represented in the male domination system.

The front line of that system in the Christmas story is Joseph, who in Matthew's account is portrayed as a liberal. Upon hearing of Mary's pregnancy by someone else, he decides not to give her the death penalty, but he does believe in the male system, and he decides to shun Mary and break the engagement. Yet he receives

---

7. Sam Levine, "Officials Defend Plan to Close Almost All Polling Places in Majority Black Georgia County," Huffington Post, August 17, 2018, *https://www.huffingtonpost.com/entry/randolph-county-polling-places_us_5b77115ce4b0a5b1febb04fc.*

a consciousness-changing vision from God, and he makes a huge shift. His maleness will not shrink if he stays with Mary—indeed, his maleness and his humanity will increase if he decides to live out of this vision rather than living out of the male domination system. Mary will need his maleness and protection in order to survive the wrath of the domination system, whether it is his refusal to ask the elders to stone her, or his willingness to help her and their son (yes, he claims Jesus as his son) escape the ravaging fury of the soldiers of Bethlehem.

This history and this biblical story give all of us, and especially us "white" folks, clues about the necessity and the nature of our resilience in engaging the system of race in our time. First, let us find ways to listen for God's voice in our individual lives, the voice telling us to look for a different story and a different imagination. This returns us to the need for recognition in our own journeys—that we are all captured by the tramping boots of domination. So we must begin with our own consciousness and recognize a thirst for the God revealed in the Jesus born to Mary and Joseph. It will be a huge step if we are able take it, and we won't be able to go back to our old consciousness if we do take this step. That's how we'll know that we have taken the step—we won't be able to go back!

Second, there is the absolute need for community, for listening to those who are oppressed. Mary found it in Elizabeth and Joseph (a surprising source!) and in Egypt. None of us are strong enough as individuals to stand up to this resistant and resilient power of race on our own. We must be in community and in solidarity with others. In this listening and engagement, we will find many struggles, but we will also begin to find a sign of life. Whether or not we will move to Mary's *Magnificat* is not as important as our beginning to believe in this alternate story of life, of the humanity of those at the margins. This shift in our imaginations is essential, because in both our discovery and recognition of our own captivity to racism, and in our continuing struggles with that power, we will need to be as resourceful and resilient as the power of racism itself.

Ida Wells understood the economic implications of the struggle against racism. The lynching of her friend Tom Moss in Memphis in 1892 was not based on the accusation that he had raped a white woman. It was based on the economic competition that he and his friends were providing in their grocery store in their black neighborhood. Their white competitors decided to attack Tom Moss's store, and when the white attackers fired on Moss's store, the fire was returned. Though one white attacker was wounded, no white people were killed. This "stand your ground" approach by Moss and his friends did not lead to acquittal—it never has when the "standers" are black—but rather to arrest and lynching. Wells quickly perceived that the terror and lynchings perpetrated by white people were based on the desire to continue to make profit off black bodies and black labor. That situation has not substantially changed, and that leads us to the fifth step in our process of seeking liberation for those of us classified as "white": *reparations.*

The idea of reparations is one of the hardest steps in this journey toward healing in regard to racism. It is so hard because it requires us to understand who the god of America is: not the God of ancient Israel or the God of Jesus, but rather the god of materialism, of money. To talk about reparations in regard to the history and power of race in American history is to run squarely into the mother lode of the false idols of our cultural life: the power of money to make us feel like somebody. Thus this step of reparations receives the most resistance by far in any discussion of steps needed to overcome the power of race, no matter who is doing the discussing.

The idea of reparations is a biblical one, as the community of Israel recognized the need to have a periodic time of reparations, of repairing. One was called the Jubilee Year (Lev. 25:1–10), and the other was an order to compensate Hebrew slaves when they were released in the seventh year (Deut. 15:12–18). This idea is based on the concept of things being broken and in need of repair. There was recognition that the necessity of reparations is a spiritual issue, and that is where we must begin our discussion of reparations.

The depth and power of the twin siblings of race and slavery are so deep that no adequate reparation can ever be made. Yet if we want to find some semblance of healing, we must wade into this area. Reparations would involve an acknowledgment of the destructive power of slavery and how much of current American white wealth was built on slave labor. It would also involve monetary payments to descendants of African American people held as slaves. It is so difficult to discuss economic compensation to descendants of people who were held in American slavery because in order to do that, we as white people would have to acknowledge how much profit we made from slavery between the years 1619–1965 (no, slavery didn't end in 1865 but rather in 1965, though it still exists in some forms). It is incalculable because so many American institutions and families were built on it. Yet we must engage this discussion, because at its heart, slavery (and the racism that undergirded it) was an economic system, building wealth for the rest of the country. The only way to begin to come to terms with this fact is to talk about compensatory payments to those whose labor, wealth, and families were stolen.

On January 16, 1865, after he had met with black ministers and other lay leaders in Savannah, General William Sherman issued Field Order #15, which confiscated some 400,000 acres along the coast of South Carolina, Georgia, and Florida.[8] It would be given to some 18,000 people and their families who had

---

8. Eric Foner, *Nothing But Freedom* (Baton Rouge: LSU Press, 1983), 82–84.

formerly been held in slavery, dividing the plots into roughly forty acres per family. Though this order was later rescinded by President Andrew Johnson in December 1865, it was an early attempt toward reparations, as the Civil War neared its end. It recognized that black slave labor had made white wealth possible. It was not the first attempt at reparations in American history. In the 1780s members of the Friends Society (Quakers) in New York, Baltimore, and New England made it mandatory for members to provide reparations to people formerly held by them as slaves.[9]

This emphasis on reparations as part of overcoming the power of racism is the part that most infuriates and mystifies those of us classified as "white." It is a nonstarter for most of us for at least three reasons. First, most of us believe that slavery ended in 1865, so how can we talk about reparations after 154 years? Second, to admit the need (if not the possibility) for reparations, we who are classified as "white" would have to rewrite our American autobiography. We would no longer be able to claim that our accomplishments have derived solely from our own individual and family hard work. Third, even if we admit the need and even the morality of reparations, how would it work in modern times?

Reparations literally means doing repair work, and in terms of the system of race in America, it means the acknowledgment by white folks (and some others) that the current economic system that exists in America was built on the labor of people held as slaves. I want to address the three main objections of white folks to reparations, to repairing race relations in America, but space does not permit me to go into much detail. For further reading, see the note below.[10] Suffice it to say that the idea of reparations is fundamental, difficult, and yet necessary.

---

9. Coates, *Eight Years*, 177.

10. Coates, *Eight Years*, 151–210; Kenneth Jackson, *Crabgrass Frontier* (New York: Oxford University Press, 1985), 197–218; Randall Robinson, *The Debt: What America Owes to Blacks* (New York: Penguin Books, 2001).

The first objection to reparations is that slavery ended over 150 years ago, and thus its effects should obviously be over by now. As we have noted earlier, neo-slavery in the South ended in 1965 rather than 1865, meaning that many people now alive lived under slavery or are first generation out from it. That makes it more contemporary and means that the problems caused by slave labor or peonage wages remain powerful and relevant. The legacy of slavery is alive and real in my generation and in my children's and grandchildren's generations. As Kenneth Jackson points out in his fine book *Crabgrass Frontier*, people classified as "black" who were able to escape neo-slavery were consciously excluded from the housing programs of the 1930s and 1940s, programs which helped to build so much wealth in white families.[11]

Secondly, if white Americans agreed to a program of economic reparations for those who are descendants of slavery and neo-slavery, it would also mean an admission that white wealth has been built on the stolen labor of people of color. This admission runs in the face of the American narrative of meritocracy, of hard work, and of individual accomplishment. Some American universities are currently being forced to make this admission, and when it has come, it has come with a gnashing of teeth. The University of Georgia, in whose state Catherine and I both live, has recently been through a long and hard process of even acknowledging that people classified as slaves or neo-slaves even worked on the campus.[12] When I have done workshops on race with "white" people, I often use a question something like this: "What would your image of yourself be if you felt that your accomplishments came not from your hard work but from

11. Jackson, *Crabgrass Frontier*, 208.

12. Brad Schrade, "After Missteps and Criticism, UGA to Honor Memory of Slaves on Campus," AJC, September 7, 2018, *https://www.ajc.com/news/state--regional/after-missteps-and-criticism-uga-honor-memory-slaves-campus/dja1Kp61WyTrzzr7BNsRkI/*.

taking the assets of others?" The almost universal response indicates that white people believe that the accomplishments of their families and of themselves are based on individual and familial hard work and sacrifice. This response fits neatly into the idea of meritocracy—those who have stuff have gotten it through hard work, while those who don't have stuff lack it because they have not worked hard enough.

Thirdly, even if we agreed that reparations are correct and necessary, how would we work it out? Would everyone classified as "black" receive reparations payments from the government? Would we have a tax added to the returns of those of us classified as "white" in order to generate the income for reparations? These are hard and difficult questions, but it should be noted that we have done reparations in recent American history. In 1988, President Ronald Reagan signed into law the Civil Liberties Act, which granted reparations of about $20,000 each to surviving Japanese Americans who had been imprisoned in this country during World War II—some 82,219 received checks. That number of Japanese Americans is dwarfed by the number of African Americans, but it does show that it is possible.

Universities like Georgetown and Yale have begun to take initial actions in relation to the profits that they made off slave labor, and while they may seem significant at the moment, they are only a small beginning. The depth of the problem is seen in this way: those involved in the discussions see significant progress being made, while those whose ancestors had their labor robbed see such actions as only gestures to make white people feel better about continuing to profit from the stolen labor. Until his retirement in 2018, Congressman John Conyers of Michigan for years introduced House Bill 40 to establish the Commission to Study Reparation Proposals for African Americans Act. It will be no surprise to anyone that this bill has never made it out of committee to the House floor.

I want to offer two solutions as beginning steps for reparations. First, there have been religious bodies in America who have enforced reparations among their membership, with the Friends Society being the most prominent. Why not require our religious groups to designate funds from our budgets to begin to offer floors of income to descendants of people held as slaves? In this sense, we would be fulfilling the biblical mandate mentioned earlier from Deuteronomy to compensate those treated as slaves. There would be many objections to this and many issues to work out, but why not start from the point that these reparations are required by the Bible and are part of the mandate of John the Baptist and Jesus? We could do that in our own local places of worship, not needing any city council or state legislature or Congress to require us or suggest to us that we do it. While I was pastor at Oakhurst Presbyterian Church, we regularly provided a floor of income to four families who were descendants of people held as slaves. We began that process by making them justify their financial needs on a monthly basis, but after a while, we decided to give them a monthly floor of income because their jobs were minimum wage, below the living level, or because their meager assistance from government programs was indeed just that: meager. It was very helpful that all of these four families were also members of our church. Fortunately, we had generous members who provided for that floor of income.

My second step is to think about a movement to amend the US Constitution to change its "three-fifths" designation for humans held as slaves and Native Americans, to restore them to 100 percent of humanity from the beginnings of this country. This would require a discussion about why the "three-fifths" clause made it into the Constitution in the first place, and such an amendment would help us reclaim the vision that all people are created equal. Such a move may only seem symbolic, but let us remember how important symbols are. And what a powerful symbol this would be—our own Jubilee in American history!

This difficult fifth step of reparations leads us to the sixth step: *reconciliation*. I don't know that Ida Wells ever experienced reconciliation with white people, although it is the place where white people always want to start discussions of racial justice. We want to begin the discussion with reconciliation, rather than encountering it at the end. As the life of Ida Wells indicates, those of us who are classified as "white" have other steps that are required of us before we can even begin to talk about reconciliation.

We will need to be careful in using the word "reconciliation" because I don't believe that those who are classified as "white" and those who are classified as "people of color" have ever had conciliation, much less reconciliation. The root of the word "conciliation" comes from the Latin "to bring together," or even "to make friends." Those who are classified as "people of color" already know that in the system of race, none of us are together, and none of us are friends. It is those of us classified as "white" who believe that we are only a small step away from being reconciled to others in the system of race, especially those seen as "black." In almost all approaches to racial justice and equity, there is often talk of racial reconciliation, and white folks especially want to move to that step very quickly, if not right away. We who are white are highly invested in making certain that other people know that we do not have racism in us, and the difficult truth is that all of us who are classified as white have racism in us. We want them to believe that we are not racist, but they already know that we are. It is not people of color who are being fooled—it is those of us who are white who are fooling ourselves. In order to have racial reconciliation, we must first have conciliation, and that is a difficult and painful journey for all of us.

In our work to find liberation from our captivity to race, all of us, but especially those of us who are white, will need to do the hard steps of recognizing that we are captives, that this system of race overwhelmed us long before we knew it, and that it will take intentional and deliberate work to begin to find some liberation. There is simply no legitimate way around this, and fortunate and blessed are we if Jesus motivates a person of another racial category to engage us and help us to move out of the captivity to race. Let no one hear that it is the responsibility of others to make us white folks engage our captivity to race. That work is our responsibility, but blessed are we when God sends us a prophetic voice of any racial classification and blesses us with the ears to hear that voice. I remember one of those messengers well.

In 2000, the Task Force to Combat Racism of the Presbytery of Greater Atlanta held hearings in various churches, asking people to testify how race had impacted their lives. All of the testimony was powerful, but one stood out for me. An African American woman, who was a medical doctor, testified about her struggles to be recognized in what was then a vast majority white, male occupation. Toward the end of her testimony, she indicated that her most anxious time now was that she was currently teaching her teenage African American son to drive. Most of us who had taught our children to drive nodded and smiled at having gone through this experience ourselves. Then she added a powerful message: "What scares me the most is not whether he'll be injured in a car wreck but what will happen to him when he has some of his male friends in the car, and they are stopped by the police. I won't be there to protect him, and I know that most police will not see him as the son of an accomplished doctor. They won't know him, and they'll see him only as a black boy, with all the negative connotations such a designation carries in our society. And I bet that none of you who are not black have ever even thought of that, of what we have to go through."[13]

---

13. Monica Parker testimony, Task Force on Racism Hearings, Presbytery of Greater Atlanta, June 10, 2000.

Her testimony struck me deeply because in the previous year, I had taught my white daughter to drive. While it was an anxiety-producing time, I never once considered teaching her what to do when the police stopped her when she was driving, without me in the car. I never considered such a lesson because I know that the system works to our advantage as those who are classified as "white." The depth of my white privilege was revealed to me yet once again, and I gained a little more understanding of Derrick Bell's prophetic quote in his 1995 book *Faces at the Bottom of the Well*:

> Consider: In this last decade of the twentieth century, color determines the social and economic status of all African Americans, both those who have been highly successful and their poverty-bound brethren whose lives are grounded in misery and despair. We rise and fall less as a result of our efforts than in response to the needs of a white society that condemns all blacks to quasi citizenship as surely as it segregated our parents and enslaved their forebears. The fact is, despite what we designate as progress wrought through struggle over many generations, we remain what we were in the beginning: a dark and foreign presence, always the designated "other."[14]

In order to do this work in regard to race, we must allow ourselves to know the vulnerability of the margins, where Jesus lives. Some of us know it because we live there, and some of us have a hard time connecting the margins with God. Why would God come to us like this? Why not as a conquering general or rich banker or powerful politician? Yet only by engaging the margins in the world and in ourselves will we ever be able to conceive conciliation in regard to race and to many other systems

---

14. Derrick Bell, *Faces at the Bottom of the Well: The Permanence of Racism* (New York: Basic Books, 1992), 10.

of oppression. Reconciliation is a long way off, because we must first engage and confront the truth that the system of race has created us to be opponents (it's not called "race" for nothing—there must be winners and losers, there must be a hierarchy). Fortunately for us, God has experienced this and continues to call us into new life. She parts the waters of the Red Sea daily—can we see them? Can we put our toes into those waters and begin to find liberation?

Here's another story to help us begin to find the meaning of conciliation and reconciliation. While I was pastor at Oakhurst, an African American grandmother came to talk with me in the early 1990s about her four-year-old granddaughter, whom she was raising. The granddaughter had attended Oakhurst all of her life, but the grandmother told me that she would have to take her out of the church. When I asked her why, she said that she was afraid that her granddaughter was getting too comfortable around white people. She had learned to be comfortable around white people at Oakhurst, and for the most part people there had tried to treat her as a child of God. When I asked her for clarity, she gave an example of what she meant. One day she and her granddaughter were in a shopping mall when a white man bumped into the granddaughter and kept on walking, without stopping to apologize. The granddaughter turned to the man and said: "You forgot to say excuse me." The white man kept on walking, but the girl ran after him, got his attention, and said again, "You forgot to say excuse me." The man huffed but did apologize and walked on.

I first heard this story as one of triumph and determination, but the grandmother had a different interpretation. Her granddaughter had learned a different world at Oakhurst—she had encountered white people as human beings, and they had treated her as a human being. Because of this experience, she expected all white people to receive her as a human being. She had lost sight of the system of race, and the grandmother felt that this was dangerous for her out in the real world of the white South—it could get her hurt or killed. I was reminded of the terrible dilemma in which people of color find themselves in our system of race: shrink back in your humanity out in the white world or risk great hurt. It became clear that this little girl had learned from her grandmother and from Oakhurst that she should choose her humanity, to refuse to shrink back from the white world.

In our discussion, the witness of Ida Wells was running through my consciousness. Though she had many internal doubts and struggles, Wells never shrank back, and I was guessing that her advice to the grandmother and to the granddaughter would be to stand their ground. I began to understand the difficulty of racial reconciliation. The choice for people of color is not whether to avoid the sting of race—that sting is its purpose. The choice is what to do with the pain. Both the grandmother and I agreed that it was preferable for the granddaughter to be hurt by her strength in standing up to the system of race rather than internalizing its debilitating demand for inferiority and shrinking back. The question was not how to avoid the pain but rather how to prepare for it and how to use it as an instrument of growth and resistance rather than as a vehicle of self-destruction. The grandmother agreed to keep her granddaughter in the church, but she also made me promise that I, as a white man, would speak out and act out so that white people would come to understand the power and destructive force of racism in all of our lives. I have tried to keep that promise.

The life of Ida Wells ran all through that process and conversation. I could easily imagine her as the four-year-old granddaughter who ran after the white man, demanding an apology from him. I heard her voice responding to the train conductor in 1884, refusing to shrink back and head to the "colored" car. I heard her speaking out in righteous anger as she published her *Southern Horrors: Lynch Law in the South* in response to the lynching of her friend Tom Moss. I heard her struggle and pain as she was upbraided by Susan B. Anthony for getting married and having children. I heard her determination to participate in the "white" part of the march for women's rights in 1913, when Alice Paul and other white leaders told her to go to the back of the march, where "colored" people were allowed to march. I heard her voice speaking up to the newly elected President Woodrow Wilson, as he contemplated resegregating the federal government. In most of these encounters, she did not win or get what she wanted, but she did not shrink back or allow white people to define her. She didn't win many victories, but she was never defeated.

When those of us classified as "white" speak about racial reconciliation, we so often do not understand what we are asking of people of color or of ourselves. Those of us who are classified as "white" must work the first five steps already outlined, and this is a difficult process. People of color must decide how much they want to engage white people on this, whether such engagement will add pain or add some balm in Gilead. Racial reconciliation is a long way off because we first need to have conciliation before we can have reconciliation. Reconciliation is so distant because all of us, but especially those of us who are classified as "white," are captured by the power of race. We who are white have great difficulty acknowledging this captivity. It is from this captivity that Jesus came to free us, but the journey is long, and the path is narrow. All of us who enter into this part of the journey should be forewarned: danger ahead, changes coming! And yet, despite my gloomy outlook, I remember that one of the promises of Jesus in John 10 is that he has come to bring us life abundant, life greater than we ever imagined!

Lest we become discouraged and overwhelmed and unable to move, let us recall that God came into the world to reconcile us to God and to one another. God came in the marginalized Jesus so that we might seek freedom from our captivity. As Paul put it in the beginning of the fifth chapter of the Letter to the Galatians: "Freedom is what we have—Christ Jesus has set us free. Stand then as free people, and do not allow yourselves to become captives again."[15]

In affluent, white dominated America, these are hard words to take and to believe. While social media has clearly documented the continued lynching of black and Latinx and other marginalized people, we in white America have tended to ask: "What is wrong with the police?" The answer is that the police are doing what we as white America have asked them to do: to keep black, Latinx, and poor people at the margins. Jesus reminds us that we are called to see a whole new world, not a colorblind world or a nonracialized world. Rather, in the midst of our kind of world, we are asked to hear and see and acknowledge that God is in the ministry of reconciliation in Jesus. In the midst of this ministry, we are called to be "ambassadors for Christ" (2 Cor. 5:20), not in the old individualistic get-me-into-heaven vein, but in the communal and eschatological vein of working for conciliatory measures of justice and equity and mercy in our lives now. God intends this work to be happening now, in our individual lives, in our communal lives, in our institutional lives. That is the work of reconciliation, and it begins in conciliation, when those of us who are classified as "white" begin to understand our "human point of view," our context of whiteness and white supremacy.

Reconciliation is a difficult process because it requires that we be able to have conversations similar to the one that the grandmother and I had at Oakhurst about her granddaughter. She had to make a decision to risk trusting me as a white man to

---

15. Good News Bible: The Bible in Today's English Version (New York: American Bible Society, 1976).

hear her concern and not reject it out of hand. I had to decide if I could hear her concern as valid. I am grateful that Ida Wells and many others had entered my life and had helped me to hear a different point of view, to help me perceive that I needed to have cultural humility. Both that grandmother and I have since departed from Oakhurst, but we remain in the process of reconciliation, because of the risks that we both decided to take and then have built on that foundation. We initially saw one another only through the eyes of the system of race, but now we are able to glimpse God's view.

That is the difficulty of the sixth step of reconciliation, and its degree of difficulty tells us why there is so little genuine racial reconciliation. Having discerned it and decided to work on it, it takes us into the seventh and last step: *recovery.*

The seventh step in our series on walking with Ida Wells on the road toward justice and liberation is recovery. Although "recovery" is a helpful word from the jargon of the addiction movement, I am hesitant to use this word in regard to racism. I am hesitant to use it because so many of us who are classified as "white" want so desperately to be cured of racism, to be able to say that it is over and done with in our lives at least, if not in the life of the world. I appreciate that desire—it is deep in my own soul. Yet I am also aware that Ida Wells has shown us that the way is narrow, and the road is long. Because of the depth of the power of race that is in us, we will never be totally free of its power. We continue to be under the "power of the prince of the air," as the author of Ephesians puts it so well in 2:2.

I do want to use the word "recovery," however, because it points us toward the goal of seeing the depth of our captivity as well as the possibility of moving toward liberation. To use the language of addiction, we who are classified as "white" will always be recovering racists. While the system of race still has power in us as individuals and as a culture, we are acknowledging it and seeking to diminish its power in our lives. The way is narrow, and the road is long.

What will recovery look like in our lives? First we must acknowledge how deeply race is embedded in our history and in our lives. I was reminded of this by another engagement while I was pastor at Oakhurst Presbyterian. One of our African American women members came to talk me about her serving on the grand jury in one of the metropolitan counties. She was still on that grand jury, but she wanted to get off of it, because the racism and language used by the prosecutors and police officers degraded African Americans, especially the references to African American women. I indicated to her that she should talk with the district attorney, and he would likely let her resign. He was an acquaintance of mine, and our sons were classmates in school. I felt certain that he would allow her to resign. She said that she would do that. About a week later, she called to tell me that my "friend," the district attorney, would not allow her to resign. He had let her know that she could resign only if she were sick or had religious objections. She had made an appointment with him to talk about her religious objections, and she had indicated that she wanted to bring her pastor to assist her in this endeavor. I was her pastor, so it was up to me. I agreed to go with her, but I felt uncomfortable with this intersection of racism and one of my white acquaintances.

When we arrived, the district attorney was obviously surprised to see me come in as her pastor—he had expected an African American pastor. She immediately noticed something that I had not—a hangman's noose on one of his bookshelves. It recalled to me the incident on The Curve in Memphis, where Ida Wells's friends were lynched in 1892, and now just about one hundred years later, we were in the district attorney's office, looking at the symbol of those lynchings that sought to strike terror in the hearts of black people in the South. The district attorney immediately launched into the reasons why the Oakhurst member would have to stay on the grand jury or be held in contempt of court. She replied that she could not serve because of religious objections to the racism displayed in the grand jury sessions. I backed her up, and with my "white" input, we began to make progress. His escape route, though, was not the racism of the system but rather her being offended by the language. He indicated that since I was vouching for her, he would see if the judge would allow her to resign. Yet he wanted to make it clear that it was because of her sensibilities rather than because of any issues in the system. While he went to talk with the judge and draw up the letter for her to sign, she and I discussed whether she should accept this or go to jail. On one level, she wanted to hold out for him to admit the racism of the system, but on the other hand, she did not want to go to jail over this.

When he returned with the letter, it indicated that the reason for her resignation was her sensitive feelings on the language used to describe African American women. We both objected to that and indicated that we would settle for "religious objections." That was satisfactory, and the letter was drafted, which she and the judge both signed. After we left his office, she said to me: "Now you get a little glimpse of the power of race in our lives. If you had been a black pastor, I would have either been in jail or still on the grand jury." I agreed and began to see the vast distance that would have to be traveled in order to begin to find some recovery from the captivity to racism. As difficult as it was in the district attorney's office, I believed that we had been on holy ground.

As difficult as it is, some recovery is possible. I have never been a big fan of the Gospel of John. Although I like many of its stories and sayings, its approach to Jesus always seems to make him too divine and ethereal. He seems so far toward the "God side" of the "two natures" doctrine that he loses relevance to human life. My discomfort with John's Gospel is deepened when I recall that it was the favorite Gospel of my home church and of many white Christians in the South. You don't see John 3:16 popping up everywhere for nothing! The divine Jesus of John's Gospel seemed to be the Jesus who denied the importance of human life and of the human dimension. Thus, white people could hold people as slaves in 1808 and in 1964 and feel like the Jesus of John's Gospel would not care.

I have been helped by the African American tradition in that Jesus takes on the suffering of the world, and if he does not dignify it, he at least is aware of it and takes it in to the Godhead, where Mother Mary weeps for us all, especially those on the margins. I've also been helped in learning to appreciate John more by two women theologians who were part of my tenure at Oakhurst Presbyterian: Dr. Deborah Krause and Dr. Susan Hylen. They helped me to see the deep empathy that Jesus has for the most marginalized of all people: women. Race is so powerful in the Western world and especially in America; poverty is pandemic worldwide, but no matter what one's category or station, there is always the oppression of women, and John seems well aware of this. As Catherine Meeks indicated so profoundly in chapter 5, Wells lived her life at the intersection of these two powerful forces of oppression.

We engage that dynamic early on in John's Gospel. In a remarkable conversation in John 4—the longest that Jesus has with anyone in the Gospels—Jesus encounters an unnamed (what else is new?) woman at Jacob's well in Samaria. This Palestinian woman reminds me so much of Ida Wells! She does not easily yield to Jesus! This is both holy and contested ground. "Holy" because it is near the site where the bones of Joseph were buried. "Contested" because Samaria is the site of the rebellion, when Jeroboam led the northern tribes out after the death of King Solomon, and the kingdom had never been reunited. So at Jacob's well in this story in John 4, we see the powerful intersection of rebellion and patriarchy. Samaritans and Jews, men and women operating out of their categories and hostilities—yet even here, there is a conversation, and there is movement.

Jesus is traveling back to his home territory of Galilee, and the journey tires him out. He stops at Jacob's well, and a Samaritan woman comes to draw water. In line with the patriarchal system of his day, Jesus asks the woman to give him a drink. The Samaritan woman, however, is no pushover—she doesn't bow to the patriarchy and give Jesus some water. Like Ida Wells, she gives as good as she gets. "Oh, so you a Jew, want me, a lowly Samaritan woman, to give you some water—is that how this works?" In his response, it is difficult to tell if Jesus is getting testy himself, or if he is testing her, or if he is inviting her into a deeper place in her life. He replies that if she knew who he was, she would be seeking the living water that he has to offer. Yet the feisty woman is not ready to yield—"Man, you don't even have a bucket—how can you get that living water?" Jesus replies that he doesn't need a bucket, because the living water that he offers will just gush up out of the ground, like a flowing fountain. And now the woman's interest is piqued—"Give me some of this stuff, so I won't have to come back here to draw water." No more serving of men.

Jesus then stings her: "Go get your husband and come back." Again, the woman refuses to yield or be defined by patriarchy: "I don't have a husband—I don't need to belong to a man to be somebody." The Samaritan woman will not allow Jesus to define her as needing a man to receive this living water. Jesus has an opportunity now to dismiss her because she has misunderstood him so much. Yet he stays with her, and he invites her into her own life. He points out the patterns of her life. This strong sister doesn't belong to any particular man, but her life reveals a pattern of needing to belong to men in general. She is strong; she is passionate, but she cannot break away from the world's definition of her and of other women: they must belong to men in order to be somebody.

And perhaps for the first time, the woman really begins to hear the invitation that Jesus is offering her. When Jesus reveals to her that she has had five husbands and is now living with another man, it is not news to Jesus, but it is news to this Samaritan woman. Jesus reveals her life to her, and she hears her life in a new way. She is known in her captivity and in her pain and in her oppression, and she is not destroyed. This sister is stunned as she receives this revelation from the enemy.

Rather than being rejected as just another captive, she is welcomed as a sister into the new life. And she becomes a great witness for the Jew named Jesus. She goes back to her Samaritan town and tells everybody about him—she is the first evangelist in John's Gospel. It is a step toward her recovery.

It is no accident that this conversation takes place on holy ground. Once these two enemies—male and female, Jew and Samaritan—engage one another in a conversation about their fundamental identities, there are great dangers and great possibilities. The dangers are seen a few verses later when the male disciples return from town and are incredulous that Jesus is even speaking to a woman, especially a Samaritan woman. The possibilities are seen as this woman finds her true definition not in the categories of the world but in relation to the One who has come to set her free from those categories.

As I think about this conversation on holy ground, I am reminded of the many African Americans and other people of color who have engaged me in such conversations, willing to stay with me and seeking to help me find my true definition as a child of God. Just as this Samaritan woman was blessed by Jesus who stayed with her and engaged her, so I have been blessed by Jesus in those who risked an engagement with me. It took me a long while to recognize that they risked a lot in staying with me and in engaging me, helping me to discern that I am more than a white male, that I am a child of God. It also took me awhile to discern that my vocation after such an engagement was not to soak up the energy and life of those classified as "black" but rather to go back into my town, as did the Samaritan woman, to go back to my people. Like this Samaritan woman, I am asked to go back to those classified as "white" to testify about our captivity to race and about the liberating power of Jesus. In order to do this, I will have to remember that for race addicts like me and all my "white" siblings, we will always need to be working the seven steps. We will encounter them again and again in our struggles with race and gender, in our search to find the liberating power of the idea of equality. We will need that quality that Ida Wells demonstrated so well: she didn't win many victories, but she was never defeated.

Questions for Further Reflection

1. Which of these seven steps describes where you are in your life?
2. Do you consider the power of racism to be similar to addiction? How is it is similar? How is it different?
3. Are you interested in using these seven steps to help you combat the power of racism in your life?

CHAPTER 7

Seeking the Beloved Community

In this chapter we will discuss the possibilities and limitations of seeking to build the Beloved Community, a phrase that is used frequently in church gatherings in relation to racial justice. We will start off with questions and then share dialogue together as our answers. In this we seek to model some possibilities for moving toward equity and justice in race relations, pointing toward the Beloved Community. The idea of Beloved Community gained ground through the ministry and vision of Dr. Martin Luther King Jr. Though it seems a simple concept, it is actually very complex, envisioning a community of people who recognize internal and external barriers to equity and justice. In this community, all are welcome to a place at the table.

Question 1: What is it about the life and witness of Ida B. Wells that gives us hope in our time?

Catherine: Wells's greatest witness lies in her sense of self and the courage that was generated by that sense. It started early in her life, as she took on the role of parent to her siblings. It is said that one has to be able to imagine what might appear impossible in order to make it possible. Wells lived out the truth of that notion. It is her lived example of prophetic imagination that can give us hope in the twenty-first century. It seems that we need to ask ourselves if we can imagine a new way ahead for ourselves as individuals and as a nation. Can we see ourselves healed and forging a path to one another across the vast divides that we have created and continue to support? Can we imagine a country without white supremacy and internalized oppression? Do we want our country to be a place where we are committed to seeing the face of God in one another or not? Wells invites us into this process of self-interrogation both individually and collectively. She imagined many worlds that were different from the society in which she lived and while that imagination was painful at times for her, she did not allow her indomitable spirit to be deterred.

Nibs: Wells had such a vision and internalized belief in equity and equality. For those of us classified as "white," she calls to us to hear our captivity to race and to engage someone who refused to even countenance the foolishness of race. She invites us into the idea of equality in a way that I had never engaged before. I want to be clear here: I don't think that Ida Wells had many hopeful expectations about white people. Her mission was not to convert white people like me. Her mission was to work for the idea of equality in the lives of individuals and for the idea of equity in institutional and structural life, in terms of both race and gender. She did this work not in the 1960s and 1970s, when there seemed to be a bit of hope. She did this work when white people were reestablishing white supremacy and neo-slavery, when the entire white system was returning to the primordial American belief in the inferiority of people of color, especially those classified as black. One of her main values to us is that she provides a framework for doing this work in a time when the question of white supremacy has been put back squarely on top of the table. That question is always a part of American history, but now the forces are regathering to seek to reestablish the truth of white supremacy. It's not quite the 1890s of Wells's time, but it's not hard to imagine that we go back there quickly. Wells's vision and determination and energy offer us a way to be authentic witnesses to the power of equality and equity, no matter what our racial classification is. To use the language of the African American spiritual, she made a way out of no way. Her life and witness are foundational for any progress that we have made, but her life and witness also remind us, as she put it: "Eternal vigilance is the price of liberty."

Question 2: Was Ida B. Wells working to establish Beloved Community?

Nibs: I don't believe that Ida Wells could even imagine the idea of Beloved Community in the sense of white and black people sharing power equally in common life. It seems to me that her main goal was to seek to establish equity in the law and in public life for black people and for women. She did believe that the idea of equality applied to her and to others, even though the Founding Fathers had intended to leave her out because of her racial and gender classifications. The power of racism was so great in her lifetime that it was hard to imagine the idea of an interracial community that welcomed all and sought to share power equally. With a few rare exceptions, all of her experiences with white people were always a fight and a struggle to establish her own right to be treated with equity and justice. Though we are far, far away from Beloved Community now, the fact that we are even talking about it is testimony to the groundbreaking work that Ida Wells and others did.

Catherine: Of course not—there was nothing in her life experience to allow her to hope that white people would begin to see black people as equal members in any of their enterprises. She forced white women into acceptance of her in some ways, but there was no effort being made on anyone's part to create a community. They had transactional relationships which helped them to achieve tasks, but that was the extent of those interactions.

As I reflect upon the relationship between Susan B. Anthony and Wells, it is clear that there was not any sense of equality between them. They transacted the business of women's rights work together, and whatever was necessary to do that work was done. For instance, Anthony fired her secretary for not wanting to do any work for Wells, but it takes more than such an action as that to create relationships of equality. Along with this I am recalling that many of the abolitionists did not want to sit on the stage with Frederick Douglass, though they were against slavery. Slavery had its own compartment in their thought process and equality had a different compartment and they were not about to allow them to be confused.

Question 3: Can we establish Beloved Community in our time?

Catherine: As I think about Beloved Community and reconciliation, I have very mixed responses to those ideas. Though my dear Bishop Michael Curry challenges us to seek racial reconciliation and build Beloved Community, I find that I do not talk about either one of them very much. When I talk about Beloved Community, I tend to think in terms of things that we have to do as a church that might allow God to create Beloved Community in our midst. I am not sure that there are many folk around who really want to make the changes that are required for Beloved Community to be born in our current church communities. I believe that acceptance of one another's stories without any desire to edit them is a major requirement of a community that wishes to be beloved. This is a difficult gift to receive. There are not many white people who can listen to the stories of black people and not feel the need to qualify the story or edit them in some way.

Nibs: This is because black peoples' stories indict white identity so strongly. Your stories (and the stories of many other people of color) expose the lies of our white narratives of innocence and self-achievement and meritocracy. It reminds me of the Canadian man whom I encountered in my Princeton lecture in 2018—he could not let the story of white racism stand, because it undercut his fundamental idea of himself. We who are classified as "white" cannot let your stories stand as they are—without our editorials—because your stories point to how captive we as whites are to racism. We also cannot acknowledge how strong you are, as individuals and as a culture, because you have endured racism and have survived and have found life. As our sister Arkanasan Maya Angelou put it: "Yet still we rise."

Catherine: I'm also skeptical because of the necessity for equity in the Beloved Community, and white power is not anywhere near ready to share power in an equal manner. Even in the more progressive churches there is an issue with the sharing of power. There will be a black person or two doing a few things, but there is a grave imbalance in the ways in which power is distributed even when the communities are intentional about trying to share. There seems to be something in the DNA of white people which does not allow them to realize that black people know how to manage things.

This dynamic is seen across all levels of interaction with white people, and most black people are very conscious about it and become very weary of it. Beloved Community demands a mutual respect and sharing on all levels that reflects the personhood of all of the folks who are involved. Thus, it means that there will have to be give-and-take in the daily round of life and work. If people embark upon this venture, they are going to be called to discomfort, as people come together with the intention of being conscious of one another and with the intent to be interested in the overall well-being of the others in the relationship. This awareness will require relenting on some things that at times might be very dear to one's heart, but needing to be let go in order to honor another person's desires or highest good.

We are not there yet. I do not know when we will be there as a church. It seems to me that the church is the best chance for this because we are supposed to have made a commitment to something bigger than our own egos. However, we have not been very willing to take this challenge on in the ways that are necessary for the creation of sustainable communities in a very widespread manner.

Nibs: It is why I put the steps of reconciliation and recovery as the last two steps in seeking to combat the power of racism for those of us who are classified as "white." We so much want to run past the realities of the power of race in our individual and communal lives, and we long to say that we are getting over racism. We want to put racial reconciliation near the first step because we do not want to have to encounter the realities that are the history of race in this country. For the seventh step, I use recovery, but I am hesitant to even use that, because I know that race and racism is so deep in our souls and imaginations that we will never fully recover from it. At one point I thought of using redemption as another step, but it seems to me that in terms of our captivity to race, the idea of redemption is not possible.

We experienced this struggle at Oakhurst Presbyterian, where Caroline and I pastored for over thirty years. We all longed for Beloved Community, but are we willing to do the work for it, especially those of us who are classified as "white"? It took me a long time in my pastorate at Oakhurst to discern two important dimensions of this question. First, I did not realize what we were asking people of color, especially African Americans, to do when we asked them to become part of the Beloved Community of Oakhurst. We were asking them to be willing to share the intimate space of worship and church life with those who had made ourselves their enemy. Second, I had overestimated the capacity of "whites" to yield power and intimate space in our own lives. We had dedicated African

American members who told me that they had to return to the black church every now and then to get a refresher on the dynamic and powerful worship experience of African Americans. Our mantra at Oakhurst was that our worship service was too white for people of color and too black for those classified as "white." My captivity to racism was so strong that it took me years to even realize what we were asking of black people and what great sacrifices that they had to make to be a part of Oakhurst. White people had to make some sacrifices too, but we got points when we could say that we were part of an interracial community of faith. To paraphrase G. K. Chesterton's comments about Christianity, the idea of Beloved Community has not been tried and found wanting—it has been found difficult and not tried.

Question 4: Given the difficulties of building the Beloved Community, are there any preliminary steps that we can consider?

Catherine: I think that it will mean that we have to be willing to listen to one another and to be in one another's presence, especially when the truth gets told, which it rarely ever does in black-white relationships. For instance, at one point in the manuscript you spoke about Thomas Jefferson, but you made an effort to make him sound a bit better than his records actually depicts. He was a rabid racist who did not believe that African Americans were fully human, yet he had one for a concubine. That historical fact has to stand and speak for itself and there is nothing that Jefferson could be credited for achieving that will change it.

However, it occurs to me that if we did not have a relationship that is striving to tell one another the truth, it might have been easier to let your observation go because it could simply be a matter of trying to be balanced. Of course, it is not a matter of trying to be balanced, it is the white person's deeply rooted kinship with whiteness that finds the need to explain the way in which whites have imagined, created, and continue to manage the world. When full acknowledgment of the indefensible nature of that system is made, it is too much of a threat to even the most progressive white people because it diminishes the power of the supremacist illusion.

Another example of a similar conversation that we had with one another was your assessment that "Wells did not win many victories." My reaction to that observation greatly interests me. In years past, I am not sure how I would have responded, but at this point in the journey I reacted quite viscerally to such an analysis because Wells's ability to stay alive for sixty-eight years was a victory. I thought about what courage of spirit and heart it took for a sixteen-year-old girl to take on the task of caring for her siblings after the death of her parents and in the midst of her own grief as a victory that cannot really be measured. There are so many instances of things such as this that one could attribute to her as victories. But if the evaluation were to be based upon the victories in the larger world of politics and economics, the picture would be different.

It was wonderful for us to talk about this and to realize the difference in the way the view appears to the white man (though progressive and liberated) and the African American woman (still pursuing healing). It is not that one is correct and the other is incorrect, actually that is mostly beside the point, the point is that we heard each other and had a conversation about the difference in the manner in which we see the world. This difference is not a cause of the parting of the way or even a heated conversation, it was actually a conversation of fascination with how different our respective responses were to the same set of facts.

I am deeply grateful that we have a friendship/relationship that can allow us to have this dialogue without it becoming confused with our standing as persons in the world. We talked about it and heard one another and acknowledged the value of sharing our understanding of how we each responded to what Wells did in the world and how the way that we assessed that speaks to the deeper issue of how we walk through the world.

It was a delightful conversation that reiterates for us the importance of this type of exchange in the process of trying to forge honest relationships across the many differences that we have. We were not attempting to change one another's view, but we respectfully paid attention in both the cases of Jefferson and the victories. In the process of doing that, we affirmed that such conversations can occur and that they can be completed without either person concluding that there is some kind of deficit in their thought processes or their personhood. There was no effort being made to set one another on the correct path, since there is not one in this case. It is a matter of the lenses created through the narratives that we have lived. While there are cases when it is necessary to bear witness to the impact of a certain narrative upon one another in a conversation, one should not avoid those instances but listen respectly and carefully.

Nibs: Those were powerful conversations, and they point me back to those first two steps that those of us classified as "white" need to take in order to have those kinds of conversations: recognition and repentance. Many of us who are white do not want to have the kind of conversation that you describe between us. We don't want to have them because we know that it will reveal to us the depth of our captivity to race. Some of us are actively in denial, meaning that we deny that racism still exists. Some of us are passively in denial, meaning that while we admit that racism still exists, it is the responsibility of someone else. To be aware of our captivity means that we are no longer innocent, a huge theme in white American history. For these reasons we do not want to have recognition of the power of race in our own lives and in the life of American society. The power of race is so great in our lives that we don't even recognize its presence—it's like the air that we breathe, to use the metaphor from Ephesians 2:2. In order to begin this journey, someone or something will have to break through so that those of us classified as "white" will begin to recognize our captivity.

The second part (repentance) is beginning to understand that there is a whole new world out there into which we are being called. Most of us who are white believe that our lives are over if we come out of denial and admit that race has power in our lives. In many ways, that is true. If we begin to have recognition, we won't be able to go back to our old way of seeing things. We'll still have many moments of the old world, but we begin to perceive in new ways. It takes many tries! I know that in my life. It has been a long journey to hear that people of color have valid points of view, that you are peers with me. And, in the matters of race, you are far ahead of me, because you have had to deal with it on so many levels that I never even knew existed. For those of us classified as "white," we must start with recognition of our captivity, and then move to finding others who can help to expand our worldviews. It's like going from a black and white photo to technicolor.

Question 5: When looking at the work of racial healing, how does one think about winning victories?

Catherine: Of course we want to see things change for the better and many of them have changed. Wells lived without seeing the major changes that we have seen, but she knew that one cannot become preoccupied with the success of the moment because this is a long journey with many twists and turns. Privilege makes it possible to engage in despair because one has to have time to waste, which is what despair causes. Black people who are conscious know that every minute that is spent in despair is a vast waste of time because there is so much to do in the struggle for freedom and time is short. So the long view is necessary and each day is crucial. For the oppressed, each day that brings any light has to be celebrated and all days—those with light and those without—have to become a part of the big picture. There is no way ahead for oppressed people except by faith and hope. Hope demands that one stays clear about what is to be done and what one has to do in order to get to the promised land and that nothing is allowed to deter the journey. Though Wells was disappointed and must have thought that the tunnel might be too long for any light to ever be seen, she had to keep going forward. If she had not continued to go forward, we would not be talking about her eighty-seven years after her death.

Faithfulness does not require success. Though we all want to see our work bear fruit in some way, the fruit may not be equal to the effort that is exerted and it is critical to work hard to keep clarity about that fact.

In the current moment, white people are far more worried about the United States than black people because nothing has changed that much for us. We have never had any illusion that the country belonged to us. Oh, for that half minute when Obama was president, there was a bit of thinking on the part of some black people that black life should be heartily impacted. They soon learned that one does not get to be president in America by having an agenda for black people. Unfortunately, this is true, and black disappointment contributed to Trump's victory because folks decided that elections do not mean anything for them. They were mistaken.

In terms of reconciliation, it implies that a prior relationship existed and in the case of blacks and whites, that is not the case. The relationships that existed were based upon the false premise of superiority and inferiority during the slave era and the supremacist myth continues to undergird much of the ways in which whites interact with black people. It seems to me that our basic hope for racial healing is to be found where white folks have

turned themselves over to God in a way for actual transformation to occur and they get led to a new place of understanding
that being a human and a faithful person is more important than
being white. Black people have to undergo transformation as well
in order to get beyond the internalized oppression resulting from
living in a white supremacist society. But this work of transformation is about healing and if that occurs, then there is a chance
relationships can be forged. Healing is the first step. If that work
is not done, nothing else of substance is possible.

Nibs: Since I'm a white male, I tend to think of victories as van-
quishing the opposition. It's taken me awhile to realize that individual and communal life are always in evolving stages, some
returning to earlier stages. When Barack Obama was elected president, it was a great surprise, and though I knew that we were not
postracial (and likely never will be), I did have hope springing
up that we had made significant progress in race relations. I had
underestimated the continuing captivity and power of racism in
America. Or, to redeem myself a bit, I so hoped that President
Obama's election was a sign that white folks might allow a black
man to have power over us. As we know, that hope lasted until
the end of Inauguration Day 2009, when the Republicans indicated that their main goal was to make him a one-term president.

The way I think now is that the engagement with racism
and sexism and other powers like these will be continuing and
complex. Victories, such as a white person acknowledging how
much race and white privilege have been a part of our lives, are
welcome and necessary at this point. Victories, such as people of
color refusing to allow racism to define their internal lives and
definitions of themselves, being recognized and celebrated by
all. In this sense, I would have to say that my concluding sen-
tence in chapter 6 was wrong. I had indicated, in what I thought
was a compliment, that though Ida Wells had never won many

victories, she was never defeated. In our conversation on that chapter, Catherine let me know that my white, male idea of "victories" was not the only perspective. If I had understood that, I would have said that one of the many gifts of Ida Wells was that though she took on the huge juggernaut of race, she won many victories, without much support. I was also pleasantly surprised that I received Catherine's comments in the spirit that they were given: edification and truth-telling.

Question 6: What would Ida Wells have thought about the present moment in our country?

Catherine: This present moment can be talked about in many ways. I mostly do not care to even think about it too much, but it seems clear to me that America is being called into being more honest because we have been hypocritical for such a long time. The playacting about liberation, caring about human rights, and all of those wonderful progressive ideas that we like to hold up were built on a shaky foundation of white supremacy that white progressives have been all right with supporting as long as it could be contained and made to look respectable.

White nationalism does not look respectable. But where were the progressives when Obama was being disrespected and racist things were being said about his family? Where were the progressives? So this present moment and its leaders are making silent voices have to open their mouths because there is a sense of horror now. Is this what America had to have in order to begin to talk about the real issues?

We do not want equality in this country. We do not want to have black and brown people in power in this country. I doubt if one could find one hundred white people who really would like to see black and brown people in charge of every aspect of running America.

Race is always at the center of everything in America. It is just at times more visible than at other times. It is the ongoing subtext in everything that is done in America, and black people have never lost their awareness of that fact. The challenge is to find a way to navigate one's life as a black person in the face of that reality. This has been the challenge since the founding of America and it will continue to be for a long time into the future. Wells would recognize the spirit that is traveling across our land at the present time because it is the same spirit that she confronted during her life time. But in spite of all of the negative energy that is so pervasive in this present moment, she would be encouraged by the passing of the first Justice For Lynching Victims Bill of 2018. The passage of this bill bears witness to the power of Wells's work and reminds us of the complexity of the justice journey's paradoxical nature. A journey that seems to be constantly interwoven with the negative and the positive, offering us a choice of choosing hope or despair. Wells lived all of her life in that conflict and she would keep choosing hope.

Nibs: The presidential election of 2016 reminded us that racism is still alive and well in the United States. I think that Ida Wells would have been shocked at the election of Barack Obama as president, but I don't think that she would have been surprised at the election of Donald Trump in response to Obama's presidency. She had no experience with any white political power except that it was oppressive to her and to her people. As Catherine stated so well, on that level, unless there are fundamental, structural changes in our society, it won't matter much who is president. Yet Wells had an indomitable spirit that was driven by a vision of justice and equity, and no matter what political winds were blowing, she would have been pushing for equity for all people, but most especially for women and for people classified as "black."

Question 7: What do you want your last word to be on the life and witness of Ida Wells?

Nibs: When I first met Ida Wells in 1985, she astonished me. Part of it was the locale of her birthplace—Marshall County, Mississippi—which is where all my forebears are from. Most of it, however, was a tremendous wake-up call (slap in the face, really) about her full humanity and about my captivity to race, which still had tremendous power in my life, even though I considered myself a progressive white person. I was stunned that I had never heard of her. Part of that was my white ignorance, but part of it was that she had almost been lost in American history. I give so many thanks to her daughter Alfreda Duster who collected Wells's biographical pages and turned them into *Crusade for Justice*. Wells had been so powerful and so threatening that we almost lost her to the men who wrote history for so many years.

She lived a powerful life and had a relentless witness. She got weary and frustrated, but she never gave up, and that complexity also attracted me to her. Wells is a powerful witness: fearless, ferocious, formidable, and feminist. In terms of the times in which we now live, she is just the witness we need to model for us the kinds of ideas and actions we should be considering and doing. As scary as our time seems, hers was much worse, and yet she persisted. Not only did she persist, she studied and challenged and cajoled and acted for justice and equity on so many levels. From taking care of her siblings at age sixteen, to her being a precursor to Rosa Parks's challenge to segregated public accommodations, to her powerful and incendiary work on lynching and its real causes, to her conversion of Frederick Douglass on that same issue, to her relentless work to end lynching, to her pioneering journalism, to her marriage and four children, to her "divided duty," to her persistent campaign for gender equity, to her helping to found the NAACP, to her social work in the Great Migration in Chicago, to her founding of many women's clubs, to her defense of so many people arrested for no other reason than their racial category, to her running for political office, to her refusal to bow to any political power or office—her name and witness run through just about every facet of justice in American society from 1878 to her death in 1931. She was a mighty, mighty witness, and we would all do well to learn from her and drink from her well of the passion for justice.

Catherine: As I think about it, Wells is ever present with me these days. I have framed photographs of her in my bedroom and on the wall at my office. She is a daily reminder to me about the necessity to stay focused and to listen for the deeper messages from what often seems like an inexplicable voice to get the guidance needed for the journey toward liberation.

Clearly, she had an internal compass that guided her along with her faith and amazing courage. It was that internal guidance that led her to step up to the task of caring for her siblings, to find a way to become employed though she was merely a teenager, to work through her identity struggles as a young woman as she worked to understand her place in the world, and to forge the path that she would follow for the remainder of her life. The message that she sends forth to me and all who are willing to hear bears witness to this force that resides in the psyche of everyone with the possibility of being activated at any point in our journey.

She was so ordinary. Yet she knew how to hold to the difficult and move through a myriad of difficulties with grace, courage, and the willingness to continue. She models how important it is not to allow our distaste for the difficult to deter us from the paths that might be unfolding before us. And she reminds all who will pay attention that we need to affirm with great gratitude the life that we have an opportunity to live in this present moment. Despite our hard times, hers were far more challenging. While we continue to confront much darkness and spiritual wickedness in high places, we need not despair because Ida B. Wells blazed a similar trail with far less resources than most of us have available to us.

She is an encourager because she did not choose the easy side of the journey toward liberation. She could have decided to live in a different manner. But she heard the cries of her sisters and brothers who had no one to speak for them. She spoke up about lynching even though it was dangerous for her to do so.

Ida B. Wells was an ordinary woman who demonstrated that there is always the possibility for one to choose the way to stand in the world and that limitations cannot be allowed to control the choice-making process. She kept resisting the forces that wanted to define her. She encountered many limiting forces along the way, but she did not allow them to have the last word regarding the direction that her life and work were to follow. She bears witness to us about faith, hope, and courage.